Heaven is for Real
for kids

A powerful way to take kids on a journey to heaven!

13 Sunday School Lessons
(for ages 4-8)

Tommy NELSON

A Division of Thomas Nelson Publishers

group.com

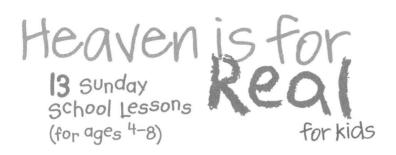

Heaven is for Real for kids

13 Sunday School Lessons (for ages 4-8)

Group resources really work!

This Group resource incorporates our R.E.A.L. approach to ministry. It reinforces a growing friendship with Jesus, encourages long-term learning, and results in life transformation, because it's

Relational
Learner-to-learner interaction enhances learning and builds Christian friendships.

Experiential
What learners experience through discussion and action sticks with them up to 9 times longer than what they simply hear or read.

Applicable
The aim of Christian education is to equip learners to be both hearers and doers of God's Word.

Learner-based
Learners understand and retain more when the learning process takes into consideration how they learn best.

Heaven Is for Real for Kids: 13 Sunday School Lessons (for ages 4 to 8)

A powerful way to take kids on a journey to heaven!

Copyright © 2013, Group Publishing, Inc.

Visit our website: **group.com**

The authors of Heaven Is for Real Ministries are represented by the literary agency of Alive Communications, Inc., 7680 Goddard Street, Suite 200, Colorado Springs, CO 80920, www.alivecommunications.com.

Credits
Contributing Authors: Stephanie Martin, Siv Ricketts, Donna Simcoe, Dave Thornton, Amy Weaver
Copy Editor: Ann Diaz
Editors: Jennifer Hooks, David Jennings, and Christine Yount Jones
Designers: Jeff Brunacci, Randy Kady, Rebecca Parrott and RoseAnne Sather
Chief Creative Officer: Joani Schultz

ISBN: 978-0-7644-9090-3
Printed in the United States of America.

10 9 8 7 6 5 4 3 2 1   15 14 13

Table of Contents

Introduction

What would you do if your child told you heaven is a real place—*and that he knew because he'd been there?*

When Colton Burpo was almost 4, he suffered a medical emergency that left him unconscious and near death on an emergency room table. Colton's parents, Todd and Sonja, were desperate. They prayed around the clock for Colton, pleading with God to save his life. They enlisted the emotional and prayer support of their church family, relatives, and friends. They began to prepare themselves for the worst.

And then, miraculously, Colton recovered.

In the weeks and months to follow, Colton began to matter-of-factly tell his parents about his trip to heaven. His statements caught Todd and Sonja off guard at first, but they just attributed it to the trauma their little boy had endured. But Colton was persistent—and he knew things there was no way he should've known about heaven. He described details that a young child typically wouldn't know or understand. He even recalled things that only have an obscure mention in the Bible. Colton said he'd met family members he'd never known—like his grandfather who died before he was born and a sister who'd died in utero. Colton's parents had never told him about his sister before.

Colton knew he'd been to heaven—and now, so did his parents.

So, what would you do if your child told you he'd been to heaven?

Todd and Sonja Burpo simply listened to Colton talk about his experience, asking him questions every now and then to hear more about one thing or another and—more often than not—to clarify that they were really hearing what they thought they were.

And Colton wanted to talk. He had some important things to say, messages he felt certain he was supposed to share. One of those messages? *Jesus really, really loves kids.*

After listening to Colton's stories and seeing his strong desire to tell people about what he'd experienced and the messages he'd come back with, the Burpos decided they would help Colton tell his story by writing the book *Heaven Is for Real*. That book has since touched millions of lives.

Colton personally knows that Jesus really, really loves kids—and he wanted to make sure other kids heard his story, too, so they would know how incredibly special they are to Jesus.

Today Colton's experience is taking on a new form to do just that. This 13-week Sunday school lesson series for kids ages 4 to 8 explores heaven in a way no other lesson book has done before. Kids will find answers to all their questions about heaven: *What's it like? Who'll be there? Are there animals there? What are angels? How long is forever?* This guide will help you give kids in your class a better understanding of our forever home.

In these pages, you'll find 13 lessons that closely follow the book *Heaven Is for Real for Kids*. Each lesson guides kids to a deeper understanding of heaven, eternity, and God by focusing in on one single Bible point.

At the beginning of each lesson, you will find helpful leader information to get you started. Objectives for the lesson along with a checklist of supplies give you an overview of the lesson. You'll also find "What the Bible Says" and "From Kids' Point of View" sections that offer brief insights on the biblical basis of the lesson and a better understanding of how kids think about heaven.

Each lesson is made up of five parts.

- **Let's Get Real** kicks off each lesson with attention-grabbing fun that'll introduce kids to the Bible point and set the pace for the day.

- **Making the Bible Real** is more than just Bible study. It takes kids on a life-changing adventure through the Bible using experiences that connect with kids.

- **Real-Life Application** lets kids take what they've experienced and apply it to their daily lives.

- **Real-Life Commitment** challenges kids to make plans and follow through on what they've learned.

- **Colton's Challenge** helps kids learn to pray like never before. Leaders guide kids through easy-to-understand talks with God.

Colton and his family want your kids to know heaven is for real. You might not be able to take your kids on a field trip there, but this guide is your next best thing.

Bring Colton and his family to your church!

Heaven Is for Real Live is bringing Colton's miraculous story to your town! The Burpos are now on tour with the band Read You and Me sharing an unforgettable worship experience at every location. Check out when Heaven Is for Real Live is coming to your town by visiting hifrministries.org.

The Heaven Is for Real for Kids app is available for download at the Apple App Store.

It's a great resource to use alongside this lesson book. Besides hearing the story read by Colton himself, the app has games and activities for your kids to enjoy.

Dear Friend in Ministry,

For the past nine years, our lives have been full of surprises and blessings. After we realized that our toddler son had made a trip to heaven and back during his emergency surgery, we have been learning from a child as he described the beauty and comfort that God has prepared for us in heaven.

Seeing heaven through the eyes and experiences of a child has inspired us as parents and now literally millions of readers as well. The accuracy and innocence Colton has displayed in his testimony has encouraged and moved people of all ages and races. But his experience definitely needs to be shared with children. Who better to describe heaven to children than another child?

Against the backdrop of Scripture, Group Publishing has created two new resources to share Colton's message from heaven with our children that "Jesus really, really loves kids."

Based on the #1 New York Times bestseller *Heaven Is for Real for Kids*, now there are two *Heaven Is for Real for Kids* Sunday school resources available.

1. Heaven Is for Real for Kids 13 Sunday School Lessons (for ages 4 to 8): A powerful way to take kids on a journey to heaven!
2. Heaven Is for Real for Kids 4 DVD-Based Sunday School Lessons (for ages 9-12): Where preteens explore what heaven is like!

These fun and effective lessons help kids explore the reality of God and Jesus, and the wonderful place they've prepared for us—heaven.

As children's ministers in our own church, we know firsthand the powerful impact that a curriculum like this can have on families' lives. We've also come to trust the proven quality of Group Publishing's material. Between Colton's story and Group's expertise, we hope you'll agree to make these resources available to the churches in your community. Thank you for being a part of this special way to share God's awesome love.

Sincerely,

Todd Burpo

Sonja Burpo

Todd & Sonja Burpo

Heaven is for
Real
for kids

Heaven Is for Real—and You're Going to Like It!

Making It Real

Kids will discover that  *heaven is for real—and you're going to like it!*

Objectives

Kids will:

- ✔ Learn about the reality of heaven.
- ✔ Enjoy acting out an anticipated event.
- ✔ Make pictures of their favorite things and heaven.
- ✔ Create heaven-bound paper airplanes.
- ✔ Think about how wonderful heaven will be because Jesus is there.

You'll need...

- ☐ Bible
- ☐ paper
- ☐ crayons
- ☐ several pairs of scissors
- ☐ pencils
- ☐ 1 copy of the "Heaven-Bound Flyer" handout (p. 14) per child, plus extra copies

What the Bible Says

Colossians 3:1

You may be wondering why you've signed up to teach 13 lessons about heaven for kids. Perhaps you've read the *Heaven Is for Real* book or seen the picture book. Maybe you're just filling in, someone handed you this book, and you don't know much about heaven. Regardless of your background, God has presented you with the incredible privilege of teaching children more about heaven.

Colossians 3:1 is a great place to start this journey together: "You were raised from death with Christ. So aim at what is in heaven, where Christ is sitting at the right hand of God." Your role is to help kids set their sights on the realities of heaven, or more accurate to the original language of Colossians, to "keep on seeking" heaven.

Since heaven is a real place, it's our responsibility to help kids understand what it is and to help them keep seeking a life with Jesus here on earth.

This book comes from the story of a little boy. Shortly before Colton Burpo turned 4 years old, he became very ill—so ill that he nearly died. The doctors had almost lost hope that he'd recover—so when Colton actually did recover, his family was overjoyed. It wasn't until weeks later when Colton began talking about what he'd experienced in heaven that his parents began to wonder what had really happened to him in that hospital room. As it turns out, Colton had experienced something that would not only captivate his family, but also the world: He'd gone to heaven and been in the presence of God the Father, Jesus, and the Holy Spirit.

You're about to lead a lesson designed to help kids focus on seeking a very real heaven today. That's in the context of a world that's very focused on seeking material treasures and gratification in this life. But Colossians 3:1 invites us to instead focus our energy and attention on seeking eternity with Jesus. You'll explore with kids how, because of Jesus, we can enjoy life here on earth and look forward to our life together in heaven. This is really the heart of the good news: We get to experience a new and abundant life in Jesus because of what he did for us on the cross, and we get to look forward to spending all of eternity with God in heaven. What a privilege we have to share this good news.

Kids learn early on how important friends and family are. They love to laugh and play with peers, siblings, even Mom and Dad. Because friendships mean so much to children, it's easy to get them to talk about their friends and to enjoy experiences together that build on those friendships. No doubt about it, even the youngest among us understand the importance of loving, joyful relationships.

Because heaven is abstract and can be difficult for kids to understand, it's important to help them learn that heaven is a real place and that it's a place they'll love. One of the big reasons they'll like it is that they'll be with their friends and family and, most importantly, with Jesus. This lesson includes lots of fun friend-focused and friendship-building experiences that'll build on kids' natural affinity for friends.

In this lesson, your kids will learn that ✎ *heaven is for real—and you're going to like it!*

The Lesson

Let's Get Real

Anticipation Pantomime

Today you'll start with a fun experience where kids act out something they're looking forward to and try to get a friend to guess what they're doing.

Have kids form pairs. If you have an uneven number of children, join in so every child has a partner. Have partners stand and face each other.

Leader tip Throughout the activities, have older kids pair up with younger ones. The older kids can help their younger friends who may not yet be reading, or who may need help understanding certain questions.

Leader tip Because every group is different, pace the discussion questions and time allotments to best suit your group of kids. We suggest always giving kids a heads-up when time is almost up so they know to bring their discussions to an end.

Say: *Heaven is for real—and you're going to like it!* **Think about something special coming up soon that you're really looking forward to, but don't say it out loud. Maybe it's your birthday party or a vacation. Choose something that you're really excited about. We're going to play a game where you'll act out what you'll be doing, and your friend will try to guess what the event is. Once your partner has guessed your event or when I say "switch," let your partner do the acting. Ready, set, go!**

Give kids one minute to act out an event and then call "Switch!" to let the other friend act out an event.

After time is up, read the following questions out loud, allowing a minute in between each for partners to discuss.

- **Tell about who you're planning to spend this special time with.**

- **What are you most looking forward to with this event?**

Ask: • **What do you think is the most fun about celebrating with friends and family?**

Say: **Today we're going to learn more about heaven and how it's a lot like the special thing you're looking forward to.**

I'm going to start by telling you about a little boy named Colton Burpo. When Colton was almost 4, he got very sick. The doctors thought it might be just the flu at first, but as Colton grew more and more sick, they got very worried. They discovered that Colton's appendix had burst and he was close to dying. Colton had emergency surgery that saved his life. But something amazing happened to him during that surgery. After Colton returned home, he began to talk about spending time in heaven with Jesus—in fact, he said he sat in Jesus' lap while his body was in surgery. Colton has said that heaven is a wonderful and comforting place where all kids are welcome.

Today we're going to explore how heaven is a real place that we're all really going to like because we'll get to spend forever with Jesus and our friends—kind of like a big party!

Making the Bible Real

You're Gonna Like It! (Colossians 3:1)

Create a drawing of someone you love sitting in Jesus' lap on a big chair. Later in the lesson, you'll show your picture to the kids.

Give a blank sheet of paper and a a few crayons to each child. Have kids each draw a picture of someone or something they love that they think about more than anything. It could be their mom or dad, a dog, a doll, a game, or even a hobby. The picture needs to be small and in the center of the paper.

Allow three minutes with a 30-second warning for kids to finish up. Then ask kids to form groups of four and tell their friends what they drew and why they love that person or thing so much.

Say: Today's Bible verse encourages us to seek the real heaven. Here's what it says in Colossians 3:1: "You were raised from death with Christ. So aim at what is in heaven, where Christ is sitting at the right hand of God." To find out more about what that means, let's think of it this way: Heaven is just as real as you and me sitting here right now. This verse tells us to "aim at" what is in heaven—but another way to say that is to "keep thinking about" heaven because it's a real place. It also tells us that Jesus is there, sitting right next to God the Father. Jesus sits there next to God just like some of you get to sit next to your dad or mom at the dinner table. Just as our home is a real place of love because we share it with our families, heaven is a real place of love because we get to share it with our families and with Jesus!

Have kids draw a picture of a big chair with Jesus sitting in it, holding their first drawing in his lap. Show kids your drawing of someone you love in Jesus' lap.

Allow time for kids to draw. Then have kids take turns showing their pictures to their groups and telling what they like best about the drawings they each made.

After three minutes, have kids add one more thing to their picture: themselves, somewhere next to Jesus.

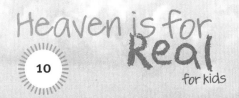

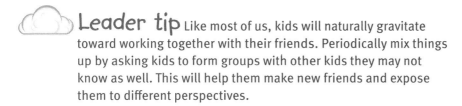

Leader tip Like most of us, kids will naturally gravitate toward working together with their friends. Periodically mix things up by asking kids to form groups with other kids they may not know as well. This will help them make new friends and expose them to different perspectives.

Allow time for kids to draw. Then have kids discuss the following question with their group.

> • **What's one thing you would like to do most with the person or thing you just drew in your picture that you can't do on earth?**

Allow three minutes. Alert kids when there are 30 seconds left. When time is up, have kids turn their attention back to you. Then ask willing kids to share their responses with the entire group. Collect the crayons to use later.

Say: The Bible tells us 🖉 *heaven is for real—and you're going to like it* because Jesus is already there getting it ready for us. We can all look forward to heaven because there are only good things there—no sadness, pain, or tears. We'll be learning much more about heaven in the weeks to come, so I hope you'll keep seeking what it'll be like with me.

Real-Life Application

Better Than Vacation

Say: 🖉 *Heaven is for real—and you're going to like it* more than you can possibly imagine! At the beginning of our lesson, you acted out something you were looking forward to. One thing a lot of people really look forward to is vacation. A vacation is a trip you take with people you love. It might be to Grandma's house or the beach or an amusement park. Sometimes people even just stay home for vacation. If you could go anywhere in the world on vacation with your family, where would you go? Shout out that place now. Let kids call out places they'd like to vacation.

Have kids form pairs. If you have an uneven number of children, join in so every child has a partner. Read the following questions out loud one at a time, allowing a minute in between each for partners to discuss.

> • **What things would you like to do on vacation with your family?**
>
> • **Describe what makes you happiest about being with your family on vacation—and why.**

Say: Let's think about heaven for a few minutes. One of the best parts about heaven is that we'll be with our families, friends, and most importantly, Jesus. Because Jesus came to earth, died on the cross for our sins, and came back to life, we get to spend forever in heaven with him. Our Bible

Get Ready

You'll need one copy of the "Heaven-Bound Flyer" handout (p. 14) for each child, plus a few extras. You'll also need crayons or pencils. You'll help kids color, fold, and then fly a heaven-bound airplane. Color and fold a sample plane in advance so you can show kids what it'll look like.

verse today tells us that what Jesus did for us is so important that he sits in a special chair right next to God the Father in heaven. Let's use the same questions we discussed about vacation, but let's talk about heaven. Read the following questions out loud, allowing a minute in between each for partners to discuss.

- **What kinds of activities would you like to do with your friends and family in heaven?**

- **Describe what would make you happiest about being with your family in heaven—and why.**

Allow time for discussion as an entire group.

Say: Remember, [pencil icon] *heaven is for real—and you're going to like it!*

Real-Life Commitment

Heaven-Bound Fliers

Say: **Heaven is a wonderful place because Jesus is there, right next to God the Father, waiting for us to spend forever with him. Going to heaven will be better than the best vacation we can imagine. Some people describe going to heaven like flying away. Paper airplanes are a good reminder of flying away to heaven, so for our closing activity we're each going to make a Heaven-Bound Flyer!**

Distribute the crayons and pencils, and have kids draw a picture of themselves and a picture of Jesus in the boxes provided. After three minutes, help kids fold their papers into airplanes. Tell them to fold along the lines in order of the numbers and in the direction described.

After airplanes are made, count to three and have kids see how far the airplanes can fly. Then have kids retrieve their planes and try again.

Say: **We can't fly our planes to heaven, but it's easy to go there, thanks to Jesus.** [pencil icon] *Heaven is for real—and you're going to like it!*

Have kids retrieve their airplanes and sit with their groups again. Read the first two questions out loud, allowing a minute in between for groups to discuss. Then read the last question out loud and discuss with the entire group.

- **Why do you think God makes it so simple to go to heaven?**

- **What would you like to say to Jesus for giving us a way to get to heaven?**

- **What are ways we can stay focused on heaven this week?**

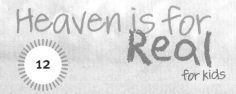

Say: Take a look at your paper airplane. Do you see how the picture of you and the picture of Jesus came together when you folded the paper? In heaven, we'll be with Jesus. In fact, he's there right now, and he's waiting for you. Remember what the Bible says in Colossians 3:1: "You were raised from death with Christ. So aim at what is in heaven, where Christ is sitting at the right hand of God."

Colton's Challenge

Closing Prayer

Say: Now that you've got some good ideas for how to stay focused on heaven this week, I want to remind you about Colton, that little boy who was so sick he nearly died. Colton says he actually went to heaven, and his message to all of us is to always remember that heaven is a real place, a wonderful place. Jesus is there, waiting for each one of us. It's going to be like one big party when we arrive!

Gather kids for a closing prayer. Explain that you'll pray part of the prayer, then kids will have an opportunity to take turns telling the times of the day they'll think about heaven.

Pray: Dear Jesus, thank you that 🖉 *heaven is for real and we're going to like it.* Help us aim at heaven all the time. Help us think about heaven when we...(pause for children to add times of the day when they'll think about heaven). Thank you that you're in heaven, sitting next to God the Father and getting heaven ready for us. Thank you that we get to spend forever in heaven together with you and many of our friends and family members. Because we trust you, we know we're really going to love heaven. Thanks for inviting us to come follow you. In your name, amen.

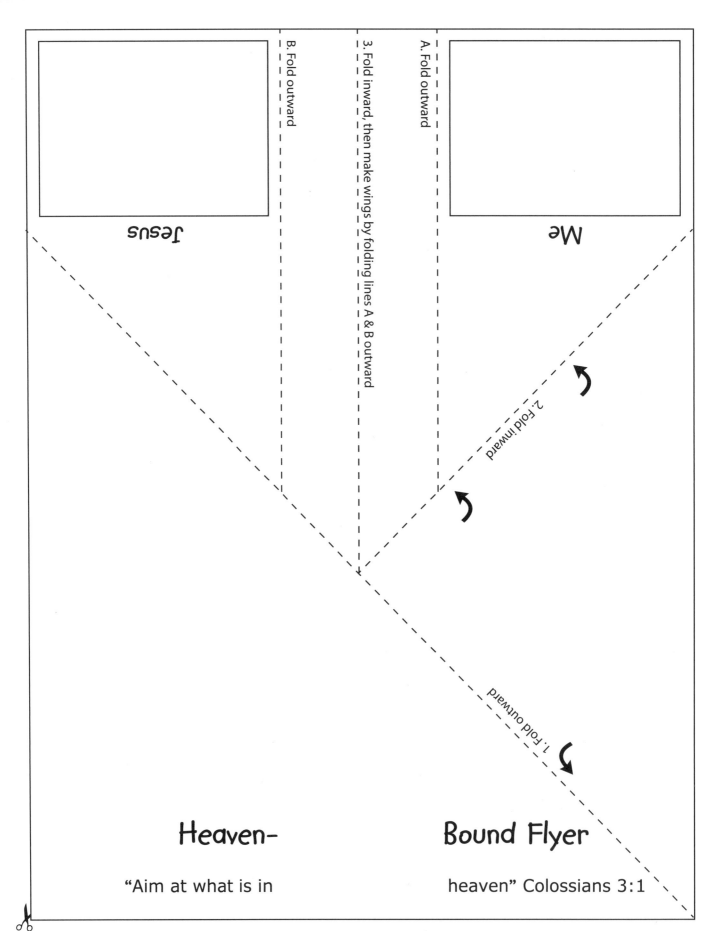

Jesus

Me

B. Fold outward

3. Fold inward, then make wings by folding lines A & B outward

A. Fold outward

2. Fold inward

1. Fold outward

Heaven-

"Aim at what is in

Bound Flyer

heaven" Colossians 3:1

Heaven is for Real for kids

14

Heaven Is a Wonderful Place

Making It Real

Kids will discover that  *heaven is a wonderful place.*

Objectives

Kids will:

- ✔ Build a model of where they live.
- ✔ Make "Heaven Is a Wonderful Place" wristbands.
- ✔ Reflect on what they like to do best in their rooms.
- ✔ Compose a song or poem about how amazing heaven will be.

You'll need...

- [ ] several Bibles
- [ ] wooden building blocks, cardboard "bricks," or other building toys
- [ ] paper
- [ ] crayons
- [ ] 1 copy of the "Heaven Is a Wonderful Place" wristband handout (p. 22) to use as a pattern
- [ ] soft fabric that won't fray easily, such as cotton flannel or low-pile fleece
- [ ] fine-tipped fabric markers
- [ ] scissors
- [ ] simple musical instruments such as kazoos, triangles, and maracas

What the Bible Says

John 14:2-3

In this lesson you'll explore with kids what makes heaven wonderful. The well-known phrase "home, sweet home" is a great way to describe heaven. In John 14:2-3, we see that it's a sweet home because Jesus is hard at work making it ready for all who believe.

"There are many rooms in my Father's house. I would not tell you this if it were not true. I am going there to prepare a place for you. After I go and prepare a place for you, I will come back. Then I will take you to be with me so that you may be where I am," the passage reads. Today you have the opportunity to help kids understand that what makes heaven wonderful is that it's our real home. Even though we all tend to think of this world as home, the Bible tells us that it's not—heaven is our real home. And Jesus is busy preparing a special room in heaven for each of us.

The other great point this Scripture makes is that there's more than enough room in God's house. That's got to be a pretty big home since billions of Jesus' followers will spend eternity together under the same roof! Jesus says he's busy working on custom rooms for each of his followers. The really amazing thing isn't just that this home for us is big enough for every follower of Jesus who ever lived, but that every single room will be specially prepared for each of us. The same Jesus who knows everything about us is preparing a room in heaven just for us. That's what I call wonderful news!

From Kids' Point of View

Kids need the safety and comfort of home. When kids feel at home they can laugh louder, play harder, and rest more peacefully. Since the world "out there" can be a scary place for kids, particularly when it comes to things like bullies, thunder and lightning, and growling dogs, they need a safe place to call home. We all remember that feeling of being scared by something outside or at school and then the relief we felt when the front door shut behind us and we felt the comfort of a parent's hug. Most kids relate easily to the idea that home is a place of safety and security, where they really feel good. Unfortunately, some kids don't have this same understanding because their home life is unstable or unsafe. If you know of a child who has such a situation at home, take care to point out to them what our home in heaven will be like. When you describe heaven, use words like *safe*, *loving*, and *peaceful*.

Early elementary-age children are concrete thinkers. Since they have a hard time comprehending abstract concepts, helping them understand that heaven is a lot like a safe, secure, peaceful home allows them to grasp what it'll be like. For most kids, knowing that God the Father is waiting for them in heaven while Jesus is getting their room ready is comforting and encouraging.

A great testament to this is that when Colton Burpo was very ill—so ill, his life was hanging in the balance—he experienced heaven as a comforting, wonderful place where his fear and bad feelings were replaced by love, happiness, and wonder. In fact, Colton even says that it was Jesus himself who brought him there specifically to comfort him.

In this lesson, your kids will learn that *heaven is a wonderful place.*

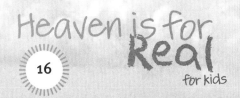

The Lesson

Let's Get Real

It's My House

Have kids gather on the floor.

Start by having kids each find a small stack of blocks to build a model of their home. If there aren't enough blocks to build a roof, instruct kids to just build the walls and leave spaces for the doors or windows. Walk around and admire kids' building projects, encouraging kids as you go. Allow three minutes. Alert kids when there are 30 seconds left. When time is up, have kids turn their attention back to you.

Ask kids to think about something fun they enjoy doing in their homes. Maybe it's playing games, reading a book, or eating ice cream—whatever they really enjoy doing at home. Allow 30 seconds for kids to think, and then have them form pairs. If you have an uneven number of children, join in so every child has a partner. Have kids tell their partners about their homes and the fun things they like to do there. Give kids each a minute to talk, with 30-second warnings. After a minute, tell kids to switch and give their partners a chance to talk.

After two minutes, call time and have pairs join with another pair to form groups of four. Read the following questions out loud, allowing a minute in between each for groups to discuss.

- **Describe your favorite room in your house.**

- **Tell what makes this room your favorite room.**

Say: **Today we're going to discover new things about heaven. The Bible tells us that heaven is our *real* home—not earth—and heaven will be wonderful because Jesus is making a special room for each of us there. And some-day, Jesus will come get us so we can spend forever with him.**

Colton Burpo, a kid just like you, knows a little bit about heaven and what kind of place it is. You see, when he was almost 4, he was gravely ill in the hospital. The doctors—and even his mom and dad—thought Colton might die. He didn't die, but he did experience heaven when his body was so sick. Jesus came and took Colton up to heaven, where he com-forted Colton and made him feel totally better. Can you imagine that—one minute being scared and feeling so sick you're near death, and the next feeling better than you ever have, sitting next to Jesus? Colton says *heaven is a wonderful place* where bad feelings and sadness go away and we're flooded with happiness and good feelings—all because Jesus makes it that way.

Set up piles of wooden building blocks, cardboard "bricks," or some other building toys throughout the room. You'll need at least 10 blocks or bricks for each child to build a simple model of his or her home. If you don't have enough blocks or bricks, kids can draw rather than build their homes.

Making the Bible Real

Heaven Is a Wonderful Place (John 14:2-3)

 Leader tip Create a sample wristband in advance, making sure the fabric and markers work well together. Supervise younger children with the markers.

Distribute Bibles, the fabric strips, and fabric markers.

Say: **We're about to discover why Jesus said heaven is going to be so wonderful. Jesus told his friends to not be afraid right before he died. This is what he said in John 14:1-3.**

Have kids open their Bibles to John 14:1-3. Have kids form pairs, and ask older kids to help their younger, nonreading friends. Have a willing child read the passage aloud.

Say: **We know that heaven is a wonderful place, because Jesus told us so. Thinking about what Jesus said to his friends, you're going to write or draw on your piece of fabric.**

Have kids write or draw things on their bracelets that could be in their room in heaven, or words that might describe their room in heaven. Remind kids that Jesus knows them better than anyone, so all their favorite things could be there. Give kids examples of what they might see when they look out their window or what might be in their closet.

Give kids five minutes to work, and provide a one-minute warning.

Then have kids form pairs. If you have an uneven number of children, join in so every child has a partner. Have the pairs share what they chose and why they chose those things.

Allow a minute or two. Alert kids when there are 30 seconds left. When time is up, have kids turn their attention back to you. Ask kids to share some of their favorite descriptions.

Let the fabric marker ink dry before helping kids tie on their wristbands.

 Leader tip As kids think about what is in heaven, you may want to talk to them about things that won't be in heaven. Colton says that when he requested "We Will Rock You," the angels wouldn't sing it!

Say: **Jesus promised us that we don't have to be afraid about the future because he's in heaven getting rooms ready for all of the people who follow him. Your wristband can help you remember not to be afraid. When you touch it, the softness of the fabric will help you remember that heaven is a comforting place, too.** Tell kids that they can remember that heaven is real and wonderful whenever they see or touch their wristband.

Get Ready

You'll need one copy of the "Heaven Is a Wonderful Place" wristband handout (p. 22). Cut out the large and small patterns on the handout. Using the patterns, cut out one strip of fabric for each child, plus some extras. You can snip into the ends to give the fabric a decorative fringe, if you like.

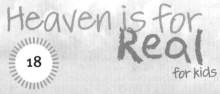

18

Real-Life Application

Heaven and Home Stories

In this experience, you'll help kids see that looking forward to going back home after you've been away is a lot like looking forward to heaven.

Say: 📝 *Heaven is a wonderful place.* **Earlier you built a model of your home. Then you told a friend about your favorite room and the fun things you like to do there. Now think about a time you were away from home.**

Have kids form new pairs. If you have an uneven number of children, join in so every child has a partner. Read the following questions out loud, allowing a minute in between each for partners to discuss.

- **Describe how you felt when you first returned home after being away.**

- **What did you do when you walked into your room—and why?**

Remind kids that Jesus said he was preparing a place for each of them. Read the first two questions out loud, allowing a minute in between each for partners to discuss. Then discuss the last question with the entire group.

- **When you get to that special room someday, what's the first thing you'd like to do there?**

- **How were your answers similar to or different from what you did and felt when you got back to your home here after being away?**

- **Why do you think Jesus would make heaven wonderful for us?**

Say: **It's amazing to realize that Jesus is making heaven wonderful for his followers. Just as our parents try to make our homes and rooms wonderful with special bedspreads, pictures on the wall, and toys, Jesus is preparing a special room in heaven for each of us. And Jesus knows us so well, he'll make it even more amazing than the way we imagine it.** 📝 *Heaven is a wonderful place.*

Real-Life Commitment

Spread the Word About Heaven

Get Ready

Have simple musical instruments such as kazoos, triangles, and maracas ready to use.

Say: 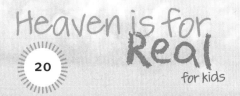 *Heaven is a wonderful place* for so many reasons, but one reason in particular is that Jesus is preparing rooms for each of us. Going to heaven will be better than the best vacation we can imagine, and arriving there will be as sweet as returning home after being away for a long, long time. Right now, you're wearing wristbands to remind you how wonderful heaven is. Let's find a way to tell others how great heaven is.

Have kids form groups of three or four. Join a group if necessary. Distribute simple musical instruments among the groups.

Say: A great way to share with others is through music. In your groups, make up a simple song or poem to tell others how amazing heaven will be! It can be to the tune of another song or a totally original masterpiece. You can use the musical instruments, clap, or snap your fingers if you'd like.

Give kids five minutes, and provide a one-minute warning. When time is up, have kids turn their attention back to you. Ask willing groups to share their songs and poems with the rest of the groups. When groups are done sharing, read the first two questions out loud, allowing a minute in between each for groups to discuss. Then discuss the last question with the entire group.

- **Describe what you think heaven will be like.**

- **Why do you think Jesus tells us he's making a place for each of us in heaven?**

- **What one thing can you do this week to make Jesus part of your room here on earth?**

Ask: • In your group, each of you brainstorm one person you can tell this week that heaven is a wonderful place—and why. Be ready in two minutes to report back to the whole group.

Allow two minutes, and provide a 30-second warning. When time is up, have kids turn their attention back to you. Ask for volunteers to share their ideas.

Say: We can leave today knowing that heaven is a wonderful place because the Bible tells us it's more amazing than we can imagine. Jesus also said that he was making a place for us there. And what Colton experienced helps us know that heaven is a place where we feel happy and all our fears, bad feelings, and sadness go away. In heaven, we get to be with Jesus in God the Father's presence—and that makes it a wonderful place.

Heaven is for Real for kids

Colton's Challenge

Closing Prayer

Form a circle for a closing prayer. Explain that you'll pray part of the prayer, then kids will have the opportunity to tell God what they are most excited for when they get to heaven.

Pray: **Dear Jesus, thank you for making 🖉 *heaven a wonderful place*.
Thank you for making a special room in heaven ready for each of us.
I am excited for...(pause for children to add what they're excited for).
Thank you for loving each one of us so much and for promising to spend forever with us. In your name, amen.**

Heaven Is a Wonderful Place

For larger hands

For smaller hands

Jesus Really, Really Loves Kids

Making It Real

Kids will discover that  *Jesus really, really loves kids.*

Objectives

Kids will:

- [✔] Sing "Jesus Loves the Little Children."
- [✔] Play a version of Red Rover that teaches them about Jesus.
- [✔] Reflect on what God likes about them.
- [✔] Share a treat and God's love with others.

You'll need...

- [ ] several Bibles
- [ ] paper
- [ ] markers and crayons
- [ ] several pairs of scissors
- [ ] 1 copy of the "Treat Tags" handout (p. 30) per 2 kids, plus extra copies
- [ ] 2 individually wrapped candies or treats per child
- [ ] a variety of craft items such as confetti, fuzzy balls, and stickers
- [ ] tape and glue sticks

What the Bible Says

Matthew 17:2

In this lesson, you and your kids will study the exciting truth that Jesus really, really loves kids, starting with a look at what Colton Burpo said about Jesus when he experienced heaven.

Colton described Jesus' clothes as brilliant white after his experience in heaven. This matches what the disciples described during the Transfiguration when Jesus ascended into heaven.

Matthew 17:1-3 offers the account: "Six days later, Jesus took Peter, James, and John the brother of James up on a high mountain. They were all alone there. While they watched,

Jesus was changed. His face became bright like the sun. And his clothes became white as light. Then two men were there, talking with him. The men were Moses and Elijah." (Note that this describes another time when visits between heaven and earth were allowed—this time, heaven-side humans were allowed to go back to earth.) This glorious appearance of the transfigured Jesus demonstrated to the disciples both the glory and holiness of Jesus as God. His post-resurrection body rose straight up to heaven. During Colton's time in heaven, he also described Jesus' ability to defy gravity as being like going up in an elevator.

Colton described Jesus' awesome qualities—a very bright white appearance similar to the sun, almost piercing eyes, and the ability to fly without wings—and said he didn't feel afraid of Jesus at all. Rather, Colton understood clearly that Jesus has a strong love and compassion for children, and he says that Jesus had brought him to heaven to comfort him. Just as Jesus told his disciples to let the children come to him during his earthly ministry, it's no surprise to realize that in heaven Jesus loves having kids around.

From Kids' Point of View

All kids long to be noticed or "seen" by their parents. You've probably heard small children implore, "Look, Mommy!" or "Watch me, Daddy!" It's a basic human need to be noticed, watched, and protected by a loving parent. It's a powerful thing to know that in heaven we can approach Jesus and have his loving, focused attention. In a world where kids are sometimes ignored or overlooked by authority figures in their lives, it's amazing for them to experience Jesus' attentive, persistent love.

You have the privilege of working with kids who naturally trust adults and who are eager to receive and give big hugs. These kids want to please you and be told they're doing a great job. They want acceptance from their peers and they want to be invited to join in. After just a little time together, you can see their innocent and pure childlike faith, evident through their actions and words. And you'll probably be moved by their words and artwork as they describe heaven—specifically their understanding of Jesus.

Colton's brief experience in heaven helped him understand clearly that Jesus really loves kids—so much so that Jesus turned his attention to Colton to comfort him when the little boy was gravely ill. All the things kids this age crave—attention, love, acceptance, encouragement, joy—await them in heaven with Jesus.

In this lesson, your kids will learn that 🖊 *Jesus really, really loves kids.*

The Lesson

Let's Get Real

Jesus Loves the Little Children

Leader tip This lesson opens with the classic kids' chorus "Jesus Loves the Little Children." If you're not comfortable leading the song, invite a gifted singer in your church to lead it live, record it ahead of time, or look for it online through a site such as iTunes. Remember: You're teaching a room full of kids who learn differently, so offering a variety of ways to learn lets all kids experience the point you want them to remember. Even if music (or art or writing or dance) isn't your preferred learning style, it probably is for at least one or two precious kids in your room. No matter what method you use to teach, have fun and pour yourself into it!

Say: *Jesus really, really loves kids.* **I'm thankful that Jesus loves kids so much! That means he thinks each of you is extra special! We're going to sing "Jesus Loves the Little Children" to celebrate how Jesus loves us. Let's stand up to sing!**

Lead kids in the words and the motions in parentheses.

Jesus loves the little children (cross arms over chest),

All the children of the world. (Cup hands together as if holding the world.)

Red and yellow, black and white (arc hand in a rainbow motion),

They are precious in his sight. (Cup hands and rock as if holding a baby.)

Jesus loves the little children of the world. (Cross arms over chest.)

Repeat the song, allowing various children to lead it with the motions.

Have kids form pairs. If you have an uneven number of children, join in so every child has a partner. Read the following questions out loud, allowing a minute in between each for partners to discuss.

- **Tell about a time you felt really loved.**

- **Our song says that Jesus loves all children. What are some ways Jesus shows love to kids like you?**

Say: ✎ *Jesus really, really loves kids.* Jesus had a very special place in his heart for children when he lived on earth. We know he really, really loves children and he's waiting for us to spend time with him in heaven, too!

Remember our friend Colton? He got to see for himself just how much Jesus loves kids. You can imagine that Jesus is pretty busy, but still he came to be with Colton when Colton was very sick. He took Colton into his arms and comforted him and let him experience the joy of heaven for a while until Colton's body recovered here on earth. That's an amazing example of how much Jesus loves kids!

Making the Bible Real

Jesus Really, Really Loves Kids (Matthew 17:2)

Get Ready

You'll lead the kids in a fun game of Red Rover to help them understand how great it feels to be "invited." Clear your room of any obstacles or hazards that kids could get hurt on as they run back and forth across your room.

Say: One time when Jesus was talking with people, there were lots of kids who wanted to be near him. Jesus' friends thought that wasn't a good idea, so they tried to keep the children away from him. But Jesus told his friends not to stop the kids; he wanted them to come to him.

Have kids form new pairs. Ask older kids to partner with their nonreading friends. If you have an uneven number of children, join in so every child has a partner. Distribute Bibles, and have partners look up and read Luke 18:16.

Say: Jesus wants to be with kids—in fact, he invites kids to be with him! Let's play a game to help us understand this verse even better.

Have kids form two equal groups, with each group standing in a row on opposite sides of the room. Have kids face the center and hold hands tightly to form a chain. As a group, have the kids step forward three steps away from the wall. Explain to kids that you'll call out, "Red Rover, Red Rover, Jesus said (child's name), come over!" and the child named will run across the room and try to break through the other group's chain. If the child doesn't break through the chain, he or she joins the group. If the child does break through, then he or she gets to take a person from that group back to join the other chain.

Play the game, letting kids say the chorus with you while you call out kids' names on either side of the room. Play until you've called every child's name, ensuring each child gets a turn. After playing, ask the group the following questions, allowing time between each for discussion.

Ask: • What was it like when you heard me call your name and invite you to come over?

• What was it like as you tried to get through the line?

• What kinds of things can keep us from breaking through the line to get to Jesus?

Read Luke 18:16 to the group again.

Heaven is for **Real** for kids

Ask: • Why do you think Jesus wanted the children to come to him?

Say: Jesus told his friends several times how much he loved children and wanted them to come to him. When Jesus was on earth, we know he really loved kids!

Real-Life Application

Jesus Loves Me

Say: ✎ *Jesus really, really loves kids.* Earlier we sang "Jesus Loves the Little Children." The song says children are "precious in his sight." That's like saying Jesus sees that all kids are special. Think for a moment about the things that make you special—maybe a special skill, a birthmark, or a trick you can do.

Leader tip Because every group is different, pace the discussion questions and time allotments to best suit your group of kids. We suggest always giving kids a heads-up when time is almost up so they know to bring their discussions to an end.

Have kids form pairs. If you have an uneven number of children, join in so every child has a partner. Read the following questions out loud, allowing a minute in between each for partners to discuss. Discuss the last question with the entire group.

- **Tell about your special talent—and if possible, show the person what your talent or trick looks like. (You can pretend!)**

- **When Jesus looks at you, what do you think *he* sees as special?**

Tell kids that they're going to find out what kind of special kids there are in the room. Going around the room, have willing kids stand and tell their partner's name and what makes him or her special. Ensure every child is introduced; if kids struggle or are shy, step in to help so every child gets an opportunity to have the spotlight.

Say: It's amazing that God gave all of his children special talents and abilities. God loves each one of us so much he wants to bless us with special gifts. Because he was kind and generous to give us those gifts, we can express our love and thankfulness to God by using those talents and gifts—even if it's a fun talent like wiggling your ears!

Real-Life Commitment

Jesus Loves Kids

Make one copy of the "Treat Tags" handout (p. 30) for each two kids, plus a few extras. You'll be working with craft supplies, so you may want to have kids work at a table.

Get Ready

Form a large circle, and have a couple of kids help you distribute two individually wrapped candies or treats to each child.

Say: **You might be wondering why you got two treats rather than just one. It's because you have a special challenge this week! We talked about the special gifts we each have and how God gave us those gifts because he loves us. We honor God and Jesus when we use our gifts. So one of the treats is for you! And your challenge this week is to watch for friends who are using gifts God gave them—maybe it's being nice to someone who's lonely or drawing a beautiful picture. Keep your eyes open and when you catch someone using their gifts, give that person the other treat and say, "Jesus really, really loves you!" Let's add a tag to the treat so people can remember why you gave it to them.**

Give each child a tag, and encourage kids to decorate their tags using the craft items you've supplied. Then attach it to the wrapped treat using tape. Give kids five minutes. Alert kids when there are 30 seconds left. When time is up, have kids clean up their area and sit down.

Then have kids pair up again and open their Bibles to 1 John 4:7. If you have an uneven number of children, join in so every child has a partner. Give kids a chance to read the passage, with readers helping nonreaders. Tell kids that just like they'll share their surprises, God wants them to share Jesus' love with others.

Say: **A great example of this is when Colton was healed and began sharing what had happened to him in heaven. Rather than keeping his story to himself, Colton shared his experience in heaven with others, and how much he felt Jesus' love. And still today, he's sharing his story with people around the world. God wants us to spread the word that ✎ *Jesus really, really loves kids!***

Read the following questions out loud, allowing a minute in between each for partners to discuss.

- **How is sharing your gifts and talents like sharing God's love?**

- **What is one thing you can do this week to share Jesus' love with others?**

Ask willing kids to share their answers to the last question with the entire group.

Have kids each think of someone in particular they can share Jesus' love with this week. Encourage kids to use their gifts and talents to show love to the person they picked. Tell kids that you will check on how things went at your next meeting.

Allergy Alert!

Be aware that some children have food allergies that can be dangerous. Know your children, and consult with parents about allergies your kids may have. Also, be sure to read food labels carefully as hidden ingredients can cause allergy-related problems.

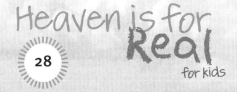

Colton's Challenge

Closing Prayer

Gather kids for a closing prayer.

Say: We're going to pray in a special way right now. I'll start the prayer, and when I say why we're thankful, please say out loud what special gift or talent God gave you that you're grateful for. Ready? Let's pray.

Pray: Dear Jesus, thanks for making every boy and girl in the whole world special. We want to say thank you right now for loving us and giving us special gifts and abilities. Right now, Jesus, we say thank you for giving me...(say what gift God gave you, and then signal for kids to do the same). Thank you that you love us so very much. We love you, too. In your name, amen.

Aren't you glad that ✐ *Jesus really, really loves kids?*

Treat Tags

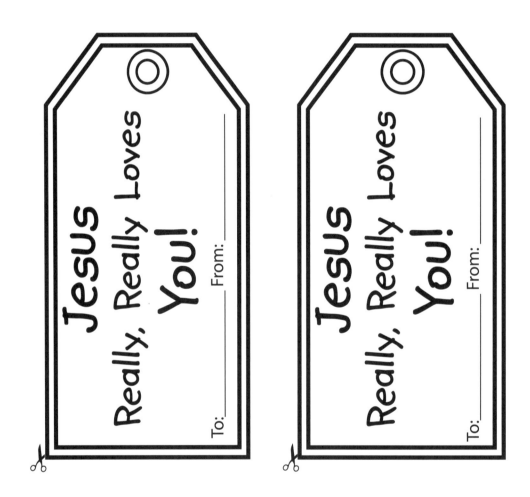

Jesus
Really, Really Loves
You!

To: _____

From: _____

Jesus
Really, Really Loves
You!

To: _____

From: _____

Heaven is for Real for kids

Heaven Is More Amazing Than You Can Imagine

Making It Real

Kids will discover that  *heaven is more amazing than you can imagine.*

Objectives

Kids will:

- ✔ Imagine the best day ever.
- ✔ Color stones to match the gems found in heaven.
- ✔ Act out going on a tour of heaven.
- ✔ Share amazing stories.

You'll need...

- [ ] several Bibles
- [ ] 1 copy of the "12 Stones" handout (p. 38) per child, printed on card stock, plus some extra copies
- [ ] glue sticks
- [ ] glitter (assorted colors)
- [ ] a soft, small ball
- [ ] crayons, markers, or colored pencils

What the Bible Says

Revelation 21:19, 21

In the book of Revelation, God revealed many things about the future and heaven to the Apostle John in a vision. One of the things God showed John was what the new city of Jerusalem in heaven looked like. John described the walls of the city as covered in 12 different precious gems and the gates of the city made of pearl. The precious stones John described roughly match the 12 precious stones of Aaron's breastplate (Exodus 28:15-21). The similarities in these precious stones symbolize that although the stones were once only for the high priest, there's no longer a need for a high priest to go to God on our behalf once we're living in heaven, surrounded by God's glory. More importantly though, the precious stones of the city reflect the beauty of God and his glory.

Colton Burpo described hearing beautiful music and seeing big, bright rainbows and shiny gems on the walls when he experienced heaven. And heaven is even more beautiful than an almost 4-year-old boy can describe and more vivid than an artist can paint. While the gemstones, gold, pearl, and glass are important descriptions of heaven, encourage kids to remember that heaven is even brighter and more wondrous than the most beautiful things we can imagine.

Use this lesson to help kids understand that until we see heaven in all its glory, we'll never truly imagine how amazing it is.

Kids have very big imaginations! Ask them what they want to be when they grow up, and they'll tell you all about being a ballerina-astronaut or a cowboy-snake wrangler. Children's imaginations at this age are blossoming as they learn new concepts and try to incorporate them into their make-believe worlds. Make-believe and pretend play aren't just for fun, though—they're actually an essential part of kids' growth and development.

Imaginative play helps a child explore his or her feelings and emotions about different situations. Children can overcome fears—like going to the doctor— through imaginative play. During the elementary school years, children begin to imagine and project through pretend play.

Knowing that imaginative play is so important, remember to nurture it as often as you can before kids begin to realize there are limits and boundaries in this world. You can encourage pretend play and build up a child's imagination by asking open-ended questions and following the child's lead. But, unlike imagining an unreal or pretend place, how much more important is it for us to dream, think, and talk about this real place called heaven? Because children don't have preconceived notions and they don't set boundaries on what things can look and be like, they may actually have much more realistic views of heaven than we can imagine. Kids can imagine bigger and brighter colors, more unique animals and plants, and more beautiful sights and sounds.

In this lesson, your kids will learn that 🖉 *heaven is more amazing than you can imagine.*

The Lesson

Let's Get Real

Best Day Ever

 Leader tip Throughout the activities, have older kids pair up with younger ones. The older kids can help their younger friends who may not yet be reading, or who may need help understanding certain questions.

You'll need a small, soft ball for this activity.

Have kids form a circle and close their eyes.

Say: **Take a moment to imagine what your best day ever would look like. Maybe your best day ever includes eating ice cream with sprinkles on top for breakfast. Or maybe rather than taking a car to soccer practice you get to ride a roller coaster to get there. Let your imagination run wild! Picture what kinds of things you would do, eat, feel, experience, and see.** Pause for a minute and then have kids open their eyes. Encourage kids to share some of things they imagined doing on their best day ever.

Next, show the ball to the kids and explain that the group will make up a pretend story about Daniel, a make-believe boy who had the best day ever because he went to heaven. Kids will make the story up one sentence at a time. You'll start the story off yourself, and then toss the ball to someone else. That person will add to the story, and then toss the ball again. Explain to kids that they should toss the ball to someone who hasn't had a turn yet.

 Leader tip During activities like this one, kids often have a tendency to only toss the ball to someone who's the same gender. If this happens with your group, consider asking boys to pass the ball only to girls, and girls to pass only to boys.

Say: **Let's start. This is the story of a boy named Daniel who had the best day ever because he went to heaven! First he...** Come up with an amazing thing Daniel did, and then pass the ball to someone else. When everyone has had a chance to add something, wrap up the story. Then ask the group:

- **How do you think Daniel's trip to heaven compares with your best day ever?**

- **Why do you or don't you think heaven will be even more amazing than you can imagine?**

Say: *Heaven is more amazing than you can imagine.* **Let's use our imaginations some more as we hear and think about how the Bible describes heaven.**

Heaven Is More Amazing Than You Can Imagine

Making the Bible Real

Heaven Is More Amazing Than You Can Imagine
(Revelation 21:19, 21)

Get Ready

Gather enough Bibles so there's one for every two kids in your group. Also print one copy of the "12 Stones" handout (p. 38) for each child, along with a few extras. Use card stock for best results.

Kids will be using glitter, so you may want to move to a space that lends itself to easy cleanup.

Give each child a copy of the "12 Stones" handout. Set out crayons, markers, colored pencils, glue sticks, and assorted glitter—the more colors the better!

Say: **In Revelation 21:19, 21, the Bible describes what heaven looks like.**

Have kids form pairs. Readers should partner with nonreaders. If you have an uneven number of children, join in so every child has a partner. Give each pair a Bible, and have them look up and read the passage.

Say: **The city described in these verses is actually heaven. Each of those stones is a valuable treasure, like diamonds. God showed John a vision of heaven, and John wrote it down so we could imagine what heaven looks like.**

Read the following questions out loud, allowing a minute in between each for partners to discuss.

- **What amazing things did you learn about heaven from this passage?**

- **How would you describe heaven to someone else?**

Ask willing kids to share their answers to the last question with the entire group.

Say: **John described the city's walls as covered in all the colors of precious stones and the streets as made of gold. Let's color our stones to look similar to John's description so we can get a better picture in our minds of what heaven might look like.**

Have the pairs reread Revelation 21:19-20. Then let kids use the crayons, markers, colored pencils, glue sticks, and glitter to decorate the stones to match the description of precious gems. Have kids imagine what color they think the word sounds like. This doesn't have to be perfect, and kids can use different colors on the same stone if that's what they think it looks like.

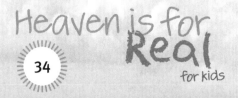

Heaven is for Real for kids

Leader tip Kids don't have to be right when it comes to choosing the colors of the stones, but for your information, here are the typical colors of the stones:

- jasper = most often red, yellow, or brown
- sapphire = blue
- agate (or chalcedony) = gray to pale orange, red, or black
- emerald = green
- onyx = almost any color but purple or blue
- carnelian = reddish-brown
- chrysolite = green or yellow
- beryl = blue or green
- topaz = colorless
- chrysoprase = green
- jacinth = yellow, orange, or reddish-brown
- amethyst = purple

Give kids time to finish coloring their stones, and provide a one-minute warning before you ask them to give you their attention.

Say: **These stones are lots of different colors. You know what else has many different colors? A rainbow! And I imagine we'll see rainbows in heaven that are more beautiful than any we've ever seen before. We'll probably see lots of things in heaven that'll be more amazing than anything we've seen here on earth. Everything will be better in heaven.**

Have kids look at their stones again. Based on the color of each stone, ask kids to think of something that color and then write or draw that item next to the gem. As they work, encourage kids to remember that the things they're writing down will be so much more amazing in heaven. Give kids the following examples to get them started: Kids might write the word *ocean* for a blue stone because it'll be bluer and more amazing in heaven. Or kids might draw a cheeseburger for the yellow or brown stone because cheeseburgers will taste so much better in heaven. Allow three minutes. Alert kids when there are 30 seconds left. When time is up, have kids clean up their area and sit down.

Ask: • **What else do you imagine will be more amazing in heaven?**

• **What do you think about heaven, knowing there'll be so amazing things there?**

Say: **It's fun to think about the things that'll be better in heaven. We can only imagine how wonderful heaven will be. The fact is, though,** 🖉 *heaven is more amazing than you can imagine.*

Heaven Is More Amazing Than You Can Imagine

Real-Life Application

Vision of Heaven

Have pairs team up with other pairs to form groups of four. If there's an uneven number of pairs, join in to make one group of three.

Say: **John gave us an idea of what the city walls and streets look like in heaven. But these verses don't describe what nature looks like, what kinds of animals we'll see, or what amazing things we'll be able to do in heaven.** Explain to kids that they are about to make up a skit. One person will be new to heaven, one will be a heaven tour guide, and the others will help act out what the tour guide is saying. Have groups discuss what they want the tour guide to show in heaven, and remind them that in heaven, everything is more amazing then they can imagine.

Allow five minutes. Alert kids when there are 30 seconds left. When time is up, have kids turn their attention back to you. Then ask willing groups to share their skits. When every group has had a chance to share, ask the following questions, allowing a minute in between each for groups to discuss.

- **How do you imagine heaven being similar to earth?**

- **How do you imagine heaven being different from earth?**

Ask willing kids to share their answers to the last question with the entire group.

Say: *Heaven is more amazing than you can imagine.* **The most amazing thing of all is that our imaginations can't even come close to how wonderful heaven will be. In heaven we'll get to experience wonderful things. And most importantly, we'll finally get to be with God.**

Even Colton talked about how amazing heaven is—more beautiful and peaceful and happy than anything here on earth. But it's even difficult for him to describe how amazing it is!

Heaven is for Real for kids

Real-Life Commitment

A-MA-ZING!

Get Ready

Prepare to share an amazing experience you've had. This will give kids a chance to come up with ideas to share about their own amazing experiences.

Have kids get into new groups of three or four.

Ask them to think about something amazing that happened to them in the past. It can be something like going on an amazing trip or seeing an amazing sunset, or even experiencing an amazing miracle.

Share an example from your life of an amazing experience. Encourage kids to shout "A-*MA*-zing!" when you've shared your story. Then have kids share in their groups amazing stories of their own. After each person shares, encourage the other children to shout "A-*MA*-zing!"

Say: **We've all seen and experienced some amazing things, but heaven is even more amazing.** Encourage kids to shout "A-*MA*-zing!" Read the following questions out loud one at a time, allowing a minute in between each for groups to discuss.

- **What's one amazing thing you're really looking forward to seeing in heaven?**

- **What amazing thing about heaven will you share with someone else this week?**

Ask willing kids to share their answers to the last question with the entire group.

Say: **Heaven is so amazing that we can't keep the news to ourselves. We can tell everyone we know. We want everyone to hear that** 🖉 *heaven is more amazing than you can imagine.*

Colton's Challenge

Closing Prayer

Gather kids for a closing prayer. Explain that you'll pray part of the prayer, then when you pause, kids will have the opportunity to finish the prayer by saying things that will be even more amazing in heaven than on earth.

Pray: **Dear Jesus, today we've learned that** 🖉 *heaven is more amazing than we can imagine.* **Help us remember that these things will be even more amazing in heaven...**(pause for children to each share one thing that'll be more amazing in heaven). **And help us remember that the most amazing thing of all is we'll get to be in heaven with you. In your name, amen.**

12 Stones

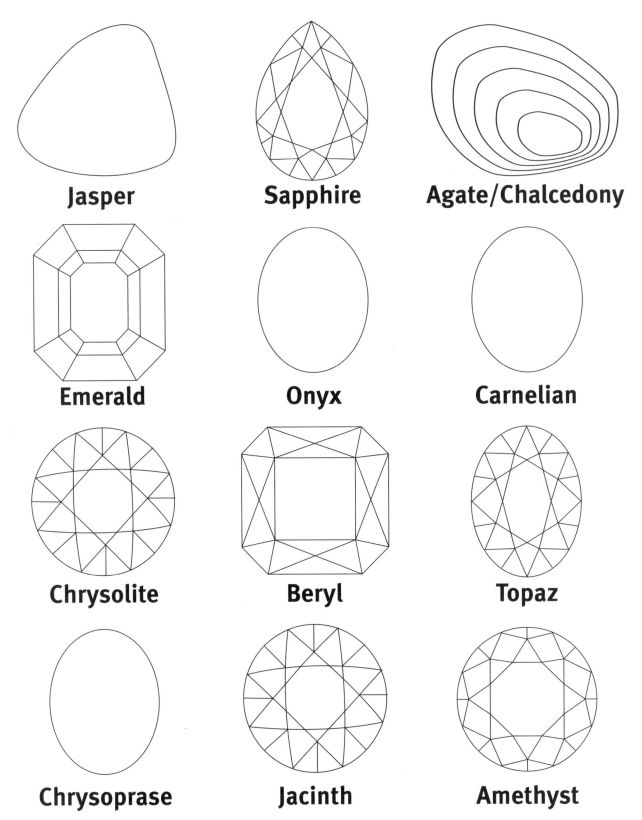

Jasper

Sapphire

Agate/Chalcedony

Emerald

Onyx

Carnelian

Chrysolite

Beryl

Topaz

Chrysoprase

Jacinth

Amethyst

Everyone Is Happy in Heaven

Making It Real

Kids will discover that  *everyone is happy in heaven.*

Objectives

Kids will:

- ✔ Create a chain reaction that results in laughter.
- ✔ Search in the dark for a Scripture.
- ✔ Decide how they feel about a variety of situations.
- ✔ Share smiley-face stickers.

You'll need...

- [ ] several Bibles
- [ ] pens
- [ ] 1 copy of the "Revelation 21:23-24 Strips" handout (p. 46) per child, plus some extra copies
- [ ] scissors
- [ ] 5 flashlights
- [ ] tape
- [ ] 2 paper plates per child
- [ ] washable markers or crayons
- [ ] large craft sticks
- [ ] tape
- [ ] sheets of smiley-face stickers (available at craft and discount stores), enough for each child to have 2 sheets of smiley-faces

What the Bible Says

Revelation 21:23-24

In Revelation 21, the Apostle John describes the exterior of the new city of Jerusalem—heaven. John explains in detail what the gates and walls of the city look like and the precious stones they're made of. The actual physical gates and walls are an important aspect of John's description of heaven because they represent entrance into heaven—and the fact that heaven is accessible. Anyone who has a relationship with God the Father through his Son, Jesus, can enter through these gates and will never be shut out. John also describes at length the walls of the city. The walls represent the safety we can find in heaven. In heaven, we're safe from enemies and evil of any kind.

During the time Colton Burpo experienced heaven, he spoke of a bright and comforting light. In Revelation 21:23-24 we see another kind of safety. Heaven doesn't need a sun or moon because God's glory lights this remarkable city. It's never dark in heaven because God's light is so bright. God's light represents freedom from darkness, fear, sadness, and death. There are no tears in heaven and everyone is happy and whole. Heaven is an amazing contrast from this life. Here on earth we encounter every kind of suffering and pain imaginable, but God promises that in his presence in heaven we'll find peace. Everyone is happy in heaven.

From Kids' Point of View

Kids this age love to laugh and are starting to develop their sense of humor. They'll often retell a "knock-knock" joke 100 times, and they're starting to pick up on subtle cues of what makes others laugh as well. Early elementary kids are no longer experiencing the roller-coaster emotions of a preschooler. Even so, just because your kids don't openly display the shifts of emotions, don't assume they aren't feeling these major shifts in mood. Watch a little closer, and ask kids how they feel—you'll be surprised at the range of emotions they express.

During these years, kids become much more in tune with others' emotions and begin to feel stress and anxiety over adult problems. They're more easily swayed by the emotions of those around them because they're becoming aware of situations outside themselves and are trying to manage their emotions based on external cues. Kids are typically able to name their emotions and connect them to specific, recent events. Because they can make the distinction between positive and negative emotions, they often want to discuss what makes them happy and sad. And they're able to express frustration over events and situations that lead to negative emotions.

Colton expressed that he was scared and feeling very terrible during the time he was ill; but when he experienced heaven, all those bad feelings fell away. He felt comforted and joyful, and even spent time with family members. This is the ideal age for kids to dig deeper into the concept of heaven, because kids truly want the joy, peace, and security that comes in eternity with God.

In this lesson, your kids will learn that ✏️ *everyone is happy in heaven.*

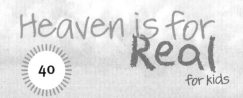

The Lesson

Let's Get Real

Belly Laugh

 Leader tip Throughout the activities, have older kids pair up with younger ones. The older kids can help their younger friends who may not yet be reading, or who may need help understanding certain questions.

Have one child lie on his or her back. Then have another child lie with his or her head on the first child's belly. Have the remaining kids each lie down with their heads resting on another child's belly until all kids are connected.

Ask the person with the next upcoming birthday to begin laughing. It'll probably be a fake laugh, which is OK since the point is to get the child's stomach to move up and down. The person whose head is on that person's stomach will feel it and eventually begin to giggle—watch and see! You'll see how one child's laughter causes a chain reaction and the other kids will start to laugh. If you have time, let kids calm down and then begin the laughing process all over again.

Have kids form pairs. If you have an uneven number of children, join in so every child has a partner. Read the following questions out loud, allowing a minute in between each for partners to discuss.

- **Tell about the last time—before today—you had a really good laugh.**

- **Why do you think this experience today made you laugh, even when nothing special happened?**

Ask: • **What things make you happy—and why?**

Say: It's so fun to have a good laugh with friends, but there are things that make us sad, too. The great news is that today we're going to discover something special: The Bible tells us *everyone is happy in heaven.* That's something to smile and laugh about.

Making the Bible Real

Everyone Is Happy in Heaven (Revelation 21:23-24)

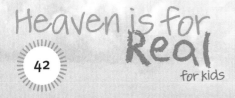

Make one copy of the "Revelation 21:23-24 Strips" handout (p. 46) for each child, plus a few extras. Cut out the sections, and tape one slip of paper to each flashlight. Hide the flashlights throughout your room.

Have kids form five groups. (Each group can be one child if you don't have many kids.) Tell them that in a moment, you'll turn out all the lights. When you do, they'll work with their group to find one of the five flashlights hidden in your meeting area. As soon as a group finds a flashlight, group members should sit together, turn on the flashlight, and have someone read the slip of paper attached to the flashlight. Be ready to help nonreaders if you have "groups" of single kids. Then they can use their flashlight to help other groups find a flashlight.

Once all the flashlights have been found, read the following questions out loud, one at a time, allowing a minute in between questions for groups to discuss.

- **What was it like wandering around in the dark, searching for a flashlight?**

- **Tell about a time you were lost or scared.**

- **How would having a light have made that scary situation better?**

Say: **Even for grown-ups, being in a dark place where you can't see what's going on can be frustrating and scary. Many times having light in the darkness makes a huge difference. Let's see what the Bible says about light in heaven.**

Leader tip Some kids may be scared of the dark or frustrated by this experience of searching in the dark. Although we want kids to connect emotionally to this experience, step in to help, or even turn on the lights if this becomes a problem.

Ask one child in each group to read aloud that group's portion of Scripture. Start with #1 and have the kids read each slip in order. Be ready to help nonreaders. Tell kids that according to Colton, it never gets dark in heaven because the light of God is so bright.

Read the following questions out loud, one at a time, allowing a minute in between questions for discussion.

- **What do you think when you hear that God is light and heaven will never be dark?**

- **If it were never dark here, what would be different about your life?**

- **How does knowing it'll never be dark in heaven change your view of heaven?**

Ask willing kids to share their answers to the last question with the entire group.

Say: **In heaven, we don't have to worry about being scared or sad or frustrated because there's no night or darkness. God lights up the city.** 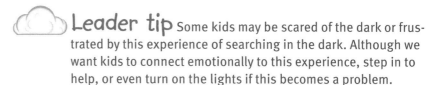 *Everyone is happy in heaven.*

Real-Life Application

Smiley or Sad?

Give each child two paper plates, a large craft stick, and several washable markers or crayons. Ask kids to draw two self-portraits—one on each paper plate. One self-portrait should be a picture of their face when they're sad and the other should be a picture of their face when they're happy and smiling.

Once kids have created their self-portraits, help them tape a craft stick to the back of one plate with a portion of the craft stick placed past the edge of the plate. Kids will then tape the other plate to the back of the plate that has the craft stick. Once complete, kids can hold up the faces using the craft stick as a handle to turn the plates so one side shows a smiley face and the other side shows a sad face.

Look up and mark the following verses in your Bible so you'll be able to find them quickly during this activity:

Revelation 21:4; Revelation 19:1; 1 Thessalonians 4:17; Job 3:17; and Revelation 7:16-17.

Say: **In a moment, I'll tell you a story about a little boy who felt a lot of emotions in a short time. Think about how you might feel in each part of the story, and then hold up either the smiley or sad face. Ready?**

A little boy named Colton was about to go on vacation. Think about how you felt the last time you were about to go on vacation. Now hold up either the smiley face or the sad face and show me those feelings. Pause.

Right before Colton left for vacation, he got so sick his parents weren't sure he could go. Think about how you felt the last time you didn't get to do something really fun that other people in your family did. Hold up your smiley or sad face. Pause.

Colton started feeling better and he got to do some really fun things like swim, visit a children's museum, and eat out. Think about when you get to do some of your favorite fun things. Hold up your smiley or sad face. Pause.

But then something happened: Colton got so sick again that he went to the hospital and the doctors weren't sure he'd live. Hold up your smiley or sad face—show me how you felt the last time you got really sick. Pause.

While Colton was in the hospital, God allowed Colton to see what heaven is like, and Colton got to meet some really special people and discover how much God loved him. How do you feel when someone shows you how much they love you? Hold up your smiley or sad face. Pause.

God healed Colton. Then Colton began telling his parents about all the great things he learned about God and heaven. Think about the last time you got to tell someone some really great news! How did you feel? Pause.

Have kids form pairs. If you have an uneven number of children, join in so every child has a partner. Read the following questions out loud, allowing a minute in between each for partners to discuss.

- **Tell about the last time you were really sick.**

- **What do you think about when you hear that there's no sickness or sadness in heaven?**

Ask willing kids to share their answers to the last question with the entire group.

Next, ask kids to get into five groups again, this time with different people. Join in if a group only has one member, and make sure each group has at least one reader.

Distribute Bibles, and have each group look up and read one of the following verses: Revelation 21:4; Revelation 19:1; 1 Thessalonians 4:17; Job 3:17; and Revelation 7:16-17. Explain to kids that these Bible verses describe heaven. As each group reads its verse, members can hold up either their smiley or sad face based on how they feel about what they've heard.

Ask: • **What surprised you about what you heard about heaven?**

• **Why do you think it's so important for us to be happy?**

Allow time for willing kids to share their answers with the entire group.

Say: **This week, use your smiley-and-sad-face plates to remind you that even though we might be sad or scared or hurt sometimes here on earth, *everyone is happy in heaven.***

Real-Life Commitment

Happiness Sticks

Give each child a sheet of at least 10 smiley-face stickers. Have kids form pairs. If you have an uneven number of children, join in so every child has a partner. Read the following questions out loud, allowing a minute in between each for partners to discuss.

• **What things make you happy when you think about heaven?**

• **Why do you think everyone is happy in heaven?**

Say: One reason 🖉 *everyone is happy in heaven* is that God gives light and joy. God doesn't allow darkness, scary things, or sad things into heaven. Unfortunately we'll still be sad here on earth sometimes, but we can get through tough times by remembering what God has promised our future in heaven will look like.

Have kids move around the room and share their stickers with other kids. When sticking a sticker on a friend, encourage kids to share one reason we won't be sad in heaven. Maybe there will be an endless supply of bubble gum or we'll never have a broken bone. Let kids continue giving their stickers away until they're gone. Have kids find new partners and discuss the following question.

> • Who is one person you can tell this week that 🖉 *everyone is happy in heaven*—and what will you tell?

Allow two minutes. Alert kids when there are 30 seconds left. When time is up, have kids turn their attention back to you.

Say: Even though we might not always be happy right now, we know that in heaven we'll never be sad again. We can share this good news with everyone we know.

Give each child another sheet of 10 stickers. Encourage kids to take their stickers home and give one to someone who looks sad or lonely. Encourage kids to tell that person that even though we might feel sad now, we can look forward to heaven because 🖉 *everyone is happy in heaven*.

Colton's Challenge

Closing Prayer

Gather kids for a closing prayer. Explain that you'll pray part of the prayer, and then kids will finish the prayer by telling why they'll be happy in heaven.

Pray: Dear Jesus, today we've learned that 🖉 *everyone will be happy in heaven*. Help us remember that we'll be happy in heaven because... (pause for children to take turns sharing why they'll be happy in heaven). And help us remember that even when we're sad, we have forever happiness in heaven to look forward to. In your name, amen.

Revelation 21:23-24 Strips

✂ -

1. "The city does not need the sun or the moon to shine on it."

✂ -

2. "The glory of God is its light,"

✂ -

3. "and the Lamb is the city's lamp."

✂ -

4. "By its light the people of the world will walk."

✂ -

5. "The Kings of the earth will
bring their glory into it."
(Revelation 21:23-24)

✂ -

Heaven is for Real for kids

You Get to Meet a Lot of People in Heaven

Making It Real

Kids will discover that *you get to meet a lot of people in heaven.*

Objectives

Kids will:

- ✔ Demonstrate unique talents.
- ✔ Run a relay race.
- ✔ Create interview questions for people they'd like to meet in heaven.
- ✔ Feel encouraged to tell others about heaven.

You'll need...

- ☐ several Bibles
- ☐ 2 individually wrapped packages of gummy candies per child
- ☐ 3 self-adhesive name tags per child
- ☐ pens
- ☐ washable markers
- ☐ a gift box or bag full of small toys to give away

What the Bible Says

📖 *John 17:24*

When Jesus knew he was about to be arrested and led to the cross, he began to pray out loud in the presence of his disciples. Jesus prayed not only for himself and his disciples, but he also prayed for anyone who'd ever believe in him. That means Jesus thought of you and the kids in your group and prayed for you hours before he died on the cross. Jesus prayed three things for people who'd follow him in the future: He prayed for your holiness, for unity among believers, and for you to be with him in heaven.

Jesus knew what he was about to endure, but he also knew what God the Father would accomplish through his pain and death. In Jesus' prayer, we see God's heart. Jesus didn't ask for wealth or an easy life for his followers. Jesus understood that this life is temporary, and he wanted everyone who believed in him to share in his triumph and glory in heaven.

Young Colton Burpo described meeting his sister and grandfather in heaven. Both his sister and grandfather died before Colton was born, but because of Jesus' sacrifice on the cross, Colton got to hug them and talk with them in heaven. Encourage kids with the fact that in heaven, we'll get to see friends, family members, and anyone else who follows Jesus.

Use this lesson to reemphasize what Jesus accomplished on the cross.

From Kids' Point of View

During the early elementary years, kids make major strides in social development. Most kindergarteners interact with others as if everyone is their best friend. Most will happily play with a child of the opposite sex and join in with a group of kids they don't know well. They aren't picky about whom they sit next to, and they're excited to be around any other child. But by the time kids reach second grade, there's a massive switch in socialization and how kids handle meeting and befriending new kids. In second grade, children are more likely to recognize personality differences among their peers, and they're more likely to become choosy about their friends. Kids will see differences in other people and are less likely to want to meet new people or form new bonds.

These contradictory developmental stages can make it difficult to teach an early elementary group of kids about meeting new friends. Some kids will look at this as a punishment, while others think the more kids they can meet, the bigger the party! There are so many different personalities and types of people, and a combination of all these will be the people we'll get to meet someday in heaven. Use this lesson to help kids grow to accept others and find enjoyment in reaching out to new people and new experiences.

In this lesson, your kids will learn that 🖉 *you get to meet a lot of people in heaven.*

The Lesson

Let's Get Real

Meet and Greet

Have kids spread out around your room.

Say: **You might know the name of every person in this room, or you might never have seen any of these people before in your life. That's OK! In a moment you're going to introduce yourself and share something most people probably don't know about you.**

Explain to kids that they'll have two minutes to meet as many other kids as possible, even if they know them already. To meet someone, kids have to find out the person's name, age, and one physical talent that he or she can demonstrate on the spot. Kids' talents might include rolling their tongues, crossing their eyes, walking on their hands, or making noises with their armpits.

After giving kids time to think about their talents, shout "Go!" and encourage kids to race as fast as they can to meet as many people as possible. After two minutes, call time. Have kids form pairs. If you have an uneven number of kids, join in so every child has a partner. Read the following questions out loud, one at a time, allowing a minute in between questions for partners to discuss.

- **What was it like trying to meet everyone and discover each other's talents in such a short time?**

- **Explain who had an interesting talent and what it was.**

- **What things do you usually talk about with someone you've just met?**

Say: **It can be a lot of fun to meet new people and learn cool things about what other people can do. The Bible says** *you get to meet a lot of people in heaven.* **Let's check it out!**

Making the Bible Real

You Get to Meet a Lot of People in Heaven (John 17:24)

Get Ready

For this activity, you'll place a package of gummy candy in each of the kids' shoes. The lesson works best if you can place the candy without kids knowing what you're doing. Hide the bag of candy so kids won't see it beforehand.

Allergy Alert!

Be aware that some children have food allergies that can be dangerous. Know your children, and consult with parents about allergies your kids may have. Also, be sure to read food labels carefully as hidden ingredients can cause allergy-related problems.

Leader tip Using an analogy of a birthday invitation might help connect kids with the idea of going to heaven and meeting many people. God the Father wants us all to join him and he sent his Son Jesus to invite us.

Ask kids to remove their shoes and place them at one end of your room. Then ask kids to gather at the other end of your room and sit down. Distribute Bibles, and pair up readers and nonreaders. Have each pair look up John 17:24. You're actually trying to stall for time while you or an assistant place a package of gummy candy in each shoe. Line up the kids' shoes in a random order, trying to keep kids from seeing what you're doing.

When the candy is in place, have a willing child read the verse out loud. Then have partners discuss the following question.

> • **What do you think this verse is talking about?**

Allow two minutes. Then ask willing kids to share their answers with the entire group.

Say: This verse is part of a prayer where Jesus is actually talking to God the Father about you and me. The Bible tells us that Jesus really cares for us and wants us to be with him. Cool, right? Let's play a game to help us understand more about what Jesus is talking to God the Father about.

Point to the shoes at the other end of your room. Ask kids why they wear shoes and tell them to think about who gave their shoes to them.

Say: You probably want your shoes back—not only because they belong to you, but also so you don't step on sharp things or burn your feet when you're walking on hot pavement. Did you know that just as someone bought those shoes for you to keep you safe and protected, Jesus bought your life and forgiveness and you belong to him? Because Jesus was willing to die on the cross for our sin, God the Father gave us to him—and Jesus wants us to be with him. That's what we just read in our Bibles.

Form two teams, and have each team form a line at one end of your room. Explain to kids that they'll get their shoes back by running a relay race. The first kids in each team will run down to the line of shoes, grab just one of their own shoes, and put it on before running back and tagging the next ones in line. Kids will continue retrieving their shoes, putting them on, and tagging the next person in line until every person has both shoes on. Have older kids help younger kids get their shoes back on as needed.

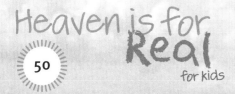

Have kids form new pairs. If you have an uneven number of children, join in so every child has a partner. Allow kids to eat the candy they discovered in their shoes as you read the following questions out loud one at a time, allowing a minute in between each for partners to discuss.

- **What were you thinking when you got your shoes back and discovered something hiding inside?**

- **Getting candy is a bonus! How is that like the added bonus of going to heaven and meeting a lot of really great people because we love and follow Jesus?**

Say: **Jesus wants you with him because you belong to him. But Jesus also wants to show you something really cool—something much cooler than candy. Jesus wants to show you his glory in heaven. Jesus' glory means his greatness and his goodness.**

Give kids a chance to look up John 17:24 again. Ask older kids to pair up with younger ones. Have kids reread the verse and think about Jesus' glory and how amazing it will be to see it in heaven.

Allow two minutes. Alert kids when there are 30 seconds left. When time is up, have kids turn their attention back to you.

Say: **Every single person who loves Jesus will get to live in heaven some day. That means there are going to be many, many people in heaven that you're going to meet and talk to.** *You get to meet a lot of people in heaven.*

Consider playing some soft music while the kids read the Bible and meditate on God's Word.

Real-Life Application

Heavenly Interview

 Leader tip Colton says when he met his great-grandfather Pop in heaven he looked like a young adult. If Colton's memories are correct, we will be able to ditch our elderly forms in exchange for something more youthful. If you have time, collect pictures of people your kids are all familiar with from a time when they were younger. Have kids guess who they are, then explain about how we may look different in heaven.

Give each child three name tags and a pen. Have kids form pairs. Try to pair writers with nonwriters so each pair has at least one writer. If you don't have enough older kids, circulate among the groups and help kids write. You can also encourage kids to draw pictures instead.

Have kids discuss the following questions with their partners.

- **Who are three people you'd most like to meet in heaven, and why?** Have kids write the name of each person on a separate name tag.

- **What's the first thing you'd ask each of these people if you happened to meet them in heaven?** Under the name, have kids write one question they'd ask that person. They can also draw a picture instead to help them remember who they'd like to meet and what they'd like to ask.

Share the following examples or come up with your own to get kids started.

Adam or Eve: What was the world like with only two people in it?

A grandparent: What was my mom like when she was little?

George Washington: How did it feel to be the first president of the United States?

Allow three minutes for kids to discuss with their partners and write names and questions on each name tag. Alert kids when there are 30 seconds left. When time is up, have kids find new partners to tell who they picked and why they would like to meet those people. Allow two minutes. When time is up, have kids turn their attention back to you. Discuss the following questions as a group.

Ask:
- **How might living in heaven with all kinds of people be different from living on earth?**

- **Why is it important to be with our friends and family in heaven?**

Say: Every person who believes in Jesus and receives his gift of salvation will be in heaven. That means 🖊 *we'll get to meet a lot of people in heaven.* We can ask Jesus' disciple Peter to show us how to walk on water, or we can talk to grandparents we never got to meet. We'll have so many people to meet and things to talk about in heaven.

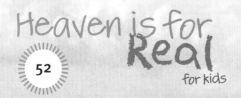

Real-Life Commitment

Free Gift!

Say: Heaven is real, and there'll be so many people there to meet and to see again. We'll get to be reunited with our family members like Colton was when he went to heaven. And we'll get to see friends we've been missing. But did you know getting to heaven is super-simple? Let's do something to see how simple it is to get to heaven.

Show your gift and say: **God wants us to enjoy heaven and be with him. But we can't make it to heaven on our own. That's why God the Father sent his Son, Jesus, to earth. Jesus died on the cross for you and me to get to heaven. It's a free gift, but it cost Jesus everything.** Hold the gift out in your hand. **Now look at this gift. This is a free gift, too. But before you enjoy what's inside, there's something you must do first. Try to guess what it is.**

Have kids guess what to do. The answer is simple: All kids have to do is come get the present from you. Help guide the kids to the answer if they don't figure it out after a couple minutes. Once the kids come to the present, give each child a gift.

Have kids form pairs. If you have an uneven number of children, join in so every child has a partner. Read the following questions out loud, one at a time, allowing a minute in between questions for partners to discuss.

- **Why do you think God the Father lets people simply take his free gift rather than making them take it?**

- **How do you feel knowing that God the Father's gift of heaven is free for you?**

- **What would you like to say to God the Father about his free gift?**

Ask willing kids to share their answers to the last question with the entire group. Then give each child a washable marker.

Say: **When we meet someone, we shake hands, give a high five, wave hello, or give a fist bump. All of these greetings use our hands. Let's use these washable markers to write something on our hands to help us remember to tell everyone we meet this week what we learned about getting to meet people in heaven.**

Wrap up a box full of small toys like a present, or put the toys in a small gift bag.

Colton's Challenge

Closing Prayer

Gather kids for a closing prayer. Explain to kids that at certain times you will pause and they can silently pray about what you just said.

Pray: **Dear Jesus, help us remember to tell everyone we meet about how to get to heaven.** (Pause.) **Please help us to make a special effort to tell this to people we meet this week.** (Pause.) **We can't wait to meet you face to face in heaven and see your glory.** (Pause.) **In your name, amen.**

Heaven is for
Real
for kids

You Will Never Get Bored in Heaven

Making It Real

Kids will discover that  *you will never get bored in heaven.*

Objectives

Kids will:

✔ Learn that heaven will be fun.

✔ Explore things that are fun to do.

✔ Create invitations to get to know Jesus.

✔ Share how they can tell their friends that heaven will be fun.

You'll need...

☐ several Bibles

☐ 1 copy of the "Ride Ticket" handout (p. 63) per child, plus extra copies

☐ battery-operated desk lamp

☐ lemon juice

☐ 1 fine-tipped paintbrush

☐ 1 copy of the "Heaven Gift Box" handout (p. 64) per child, plus extra copies

☐ washable markers

☐ several pairs of scissors

☐ stickers

☐ tape

What the Bible Says

📖 *Mark 10:14-16*

The Bible makes it clear that God really loves kids. In fact, Mark 10:15 says, "I tell you the truth. You must accept the kingdom of God as a little child accepts things, or you will never enter it." You might hear kids say they're afraid heaven will be boring—it's for eternity, after all—but would a God who loves kids so much create a place where they wouldn't be happy?

Colton Burpo experienced heaven before he turned 4 years old, when he nearly died due to a burst appendix. After he healed, Colton told his mom and dad how happy he was to see lots of kids in heaven playing games and having fun. Kids love to have fun! Jesus wants kids to come to him, so God has created heaven to be a fun and exciting place where children would want to go.

Luke 15:7 says, "In the same way, I tell you there is much joy in heaven when one sinner changes his heart. There is more joy for that one sinner than there is for 99 good people who don't need to change." There is joy in heaven! Can you imagine being in a place where happiness doesn't end? Revelation 21:4 tells us, "He will wipe away every tear from their eyes. There will be no more death, sadness, crying, or pain. All the old ways are gone." Heaven is a place that's all good! This lesson will help kids understand that, be excited by it, and want to invite their friends to come along.

In Mark 10:14-16, we read that everyone wanted to see Jesus. Parents wanted to bring their kids to see Jesus so that he could touch them and bless them. The disciples, thinking they were protecting Jesus from what they probably considered "bothersome" kids, scolded the parents and told them not to bother Jesus.

But Jesus saw this and got mad at his disciples—and they got a scolding! Jesus wanted kids to come to him. Jesus said that anyone who doesn't receive the kingdom of God like a child would never enter it. Then Jesus did just what the parents wanted him to do; he gathered the kids into his arms, placed his hands on their heads, and blessed them.

From Kids' Point of View

All too often, kids hear a warning from parents not to be a bother. This is especially true at church. Well-meaning parents will say things like, "Sit there and be quiet." The downside of this is children start to think that they will be a bother in heaven, which is not the case.

Here's a sad truth: When most kids think of "big" church, they think of someplace boring. They may picture sitting in a pew or a chair with their parents, singing boring songs they don't like, and getting fidgety during the boring message they don't understand. They may have their minds on what they're going to do *after* church—who they're going to play with, what they're going to eat, and where they're going to go.

When it comes to heaven, kids might picture it being "churchy," where they have to sing songs with no motions, listen to a minister talk about things they don't understand, and think about the fact that they'd much rather be playing with their friends.

If your kids think like that, get ready for a change. In this lesson, your kids will learn that 🖉 *you will never get bored in heaven.*

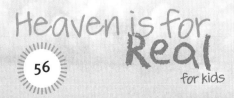

The Lesson

Let's Get Real

Ticket to Ride

 Leader tip Throughout the activities, have older kids pair up with younger ones. The older kids can help their younger friends who may not yet be reading, or who may need help understanding certain questions.

Have kids line up behind you, and tell them to follow you in a straight line. Walk slowly around the room with your arms at your sides. Make one lap around the room, then come to a stop.

Then tell kids that they'll go around the room again, but this time they're going to pretend they're at an amusement park and about to get on an exciting roller coaster. At this point, talk like you're an excited amusement park worker.

Say: **Welcome, everybody, to the greatest roller coaster ride ever! Everyone line up! Do you have your tickets ready?**

Wait for kids to say they don't have any tickets, and then say: **Oh my! I totally forgot to give them to you!**

Hand each child a ticket, and have kids line up again. Say: **Now if you want to ride the roller coaster, I need you to show me your tickets.**

Let kids hold up their tickets, and then tell them to get on the coaster. Instruct kids to pull down their safety bars and hold on tight. Then lead kids around the room again. This time make different turns and squat up and down like a roller coaster—and go fast! Lead kids around the room several times, and then stop.

Have kids form pairs. If you have an uneven number of children, join in so every child has a partner. Read the following questions out loud, allowing a minute in between each for partners to discuss.

- **What was different about our two trips around the room?**

- **Which trip was more fun—and why?**

Ask willing kids to share their answers to the last question with the entire group.

Say: **Our trip on the roller coaster is kind of like how it'll be in heaven—there'll be too much fun, exciting stuff happening for it to be boring.** *You will never get bored in heaven!*

Thank kids for riding the amazing roller coaster, and remind them to keep their tickets since they'll need them later in the lesson. Distribute Bibles.

Get Ready

You'll need one copy of the "Ride Ticket" handout (p. 63) for each child, plus a few extras. Before the lesson, use lemon juice and a fine-tipped paintbrush to write the word *Jesus* on each ticket. The message should dry clear, and will appear later on in the lesson. Place chairs for kids to wind around or climb over during the roller coaster portion of this activity. Another option is to go to a playground and slide down a slide, swing on a swing, and travel across monkey bars.

Making the Bible Real

You'll Never Get Bored in Heaven (Mark 10:14-16)

Get Ready

Kids will each need a "Ride Ticket" from the previous activity. You'll give these to kids so they can "enter" heaven. Have a few extra copies on hand in case they're damaged during your roller coaster ride. Also make sure that you've cleared any obstacles from one area of your room, where kids will try to get closer to Jesus in a game.

Say: **Jesus loves children and he wants to be around you. He loves to see you have fun and play. There was a time that Jesus was frustrated by his disciples because they wouldn't let children come to him. Let's open our Bibles to Mark 10:14-16 and see what happened that day.** Pair readers with nonreaders, and help kids find the passage in their Bibles. Ask willing kids to read each verse.

Tell kids that they're going to pretend they see Jesus in the room, just like the children in the Bible saw him. Choose an area of the room that's open and free of obstacles. Have kids show you how they would go to see him. They can run, hop, skip, jump, or even roll to get close to Jesus.

Say: **After the kids finally got to Jesus, he put his hands on them and blessed them.** As you say this, walk around and gently touch each child on the shoulder.

Say: **Jesus also told his disciples that to enter heaven, people need to be a lot more like you kids. Let's pretend we're going to enter heaven.** Lead kids out of your room, and close the door. Then tell kids that heaven is inside the room. Tell kids that to enter heaven, they will need something special. Hold a play auction for a ticket into heaven. Have kids say what they would give to get a ticket into heaven. It can be their shoes, their hat, anything they have. After a while, explain to kids that nothing they have could buy a ticket into heaven.

Turn on your lamp, and ask kids to get out their ride tickets. Tell kids to hold up their tickets close to the bulb. The heat should reveal the name *Jesus*. Let kids pretend they're entering heaven for the first time once they see the message. When everyone is back in your room, say: **Jesus is how we get to heaven. We can't make it to heaven on our own, so he paid the price for us. He really loves children and he wants you to be happy forever. Remember, 🖉 *you will never get bored in heaven.***

Have kids form pairs. If you have an uneven number of children, join in so every child has a partner. Read the following questions out loud, one at a time, allowing a minute in between questions for partners to discuss.

- **Tell about a time you received a cool gift.**

- **How is heaven like a gift?**

- **Tell about one thing you're really looking forward to about heaven.**

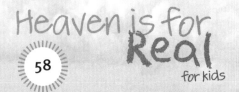

Ask willing kids to share their answers to the last question with the entire group.

Say: **All you need to get into heaven is to ask Jesus into your heart. That's the ticket to heaven! It's a gift from God, and it's *really that simple*. Who's excited to go to heaven and see Jesus?** Encourage kids to jump up and down, hoot and holler, and clap to show their excitement about seeing Jesus in heaven. Tease your group a couple of times by telling them you can't hear them. Let kids get noisy, and encourage their excited response.

Say: **Wave your ticket in the air so I know you're ready to hang out with Jesus in heaven!** Let kids wave their tickets.

Leader tip If you have kids who want to follow Jesus, this is the perfect opportunity! Simply lead these kids in prayer, saying: Jesus, thank you for dying on the cross for my sins. I believe you died and came back to life again for me. Please forgive me of my sins so I can be with you in heaven. In your name, amen.

Say: **We're going to make something to help you share with your friends the good news that** 🖉 *you will never get bored in heaven.*

 Get Ready

During this activity, kids will create gift boxes to share with their friends. You'll need one copy of the "Heaven Gift Box" handout (p. 64) per child, plus a few extras. Set out scissors, stickers, markers, and tape. You may want to move to an area with tables for this craft, or let kids work on the floor.

Make a sample in advance to show kids.

Real-Life Application

Heavenly Invitation

☁ Leader tip You can make extra copies of the gift box hand-out to give kids so they can make more invitations at home for their friends.

Say: **It's important to share with others that heaven is a free gift! Today you will each get to make a very special invitation to heaven for one of your friends, in the form of a gift box.** Show kids the sample Heaven Gift Box you made.

Give each child a handout, markers, scissors, tape, and stickers. Demonstrate how to cut along the dotted lines, fold the solid lines inward, and tape the box according to the directions on the handout. Help as needed. Then have the kids decorate their boxes. As kids work, encourage each of them to think about who they want to give their gift box to.

Once they're finished, have them write *Free gift!* on the box. Older kids can help younger kids.

Say: 🖉 *You will never get bored in heaven!* **It's an amazing gift, and thanks to Jesus, it's free! Using this box, you can tell others about the free gift of heaven as well!**

Have kids form pairs. If you have an uneven number of children, join in so every child has a partner. Read the following questions out loud, allowing a minute in between each for partners to discuss.

• **What would you like best about having your friends in heaven with you?**

• **Why is it important to invite your friends to come with you to heaven?**

Ask willing kids to share their answers to the last question with the entire group.

Say: **When you go home today, you can give the gift box you made to a special friend. When you give the gift, remind your friend that** 🖉 *you will never get bored in heaven!*

Heaven is for Real for kids

Real-Life Commitment

No Boredom Allowed

 Leader tip Do you really want to excite your kids about heaven? Tell them to get ready to fly! Colton says that in heaven we won't be angels, but we will have wings like them. If Colton's memories are correct, imagine how fun that will be. Ask your kids if they would like to try flying!

Say: **Jesus wants all children to come to him. That includes your friends. That's so exciting! It's like Jesus is throwing a big party for all kids, just like he did for little Colton when he visited heaven. Heaven is a place where amazing, wonderful, exciting things are happening, and nothing is impossible. It's so much more exciting than the best roller coaster in the world. That's why Colton is still talking about it even though he's now much older. In heaven, there's no such thing as boredom!**

Have partners brainstorm some of the most boring things they have to do here on earth. Once they have three boring things, have them come up with ways those boring things might become really exciting in heaven. For instance, kids might say homework is really boring. In heaven, though, they might do homework in a golden park with trees as tall as clouds, where the grass grows back as fast as you pull it.

Allow two minutes. When one minute is left, have partners swap roles. When time is up, have kids turn their attention back to you.

Ask: • **Why do you think Jesus cares so much about making heaven a great place for everyone?**

• **Why do you think some people think heaven will be boring?**

• **How can you tell a friend about how much Jesus cares for each of us?**

Allow time for discussion.

Colton's Challenge

Closing Prayer

Have kids form a circle.

Say: **Just like we invite people to come to a party, we can invite people to learn about what an amazing, exciting place heaven is.** Have kids find their tickets from the roller coaster ride and give them each something to write with. **Let's all take a quiet moment and sit still, holding our tickets. Close your eyes and silently ask God to help you think of the right person to tell about heaven this week.**

After 30 seconds, explain that you'll pray part of the closing prayer, and then on your cue, kids will each write the name of the friend they're going to invite this week to come to accept the free gift of heaven.

Pray: **Dear Jesus, today we've learned that** *we will never get bored in heaven.* **Help us share that good news with our friends…**(pause for kids to write the name of a friend). **Thank you for welcoming all kids to come to you. In your name, amen.**

Ride Ticket

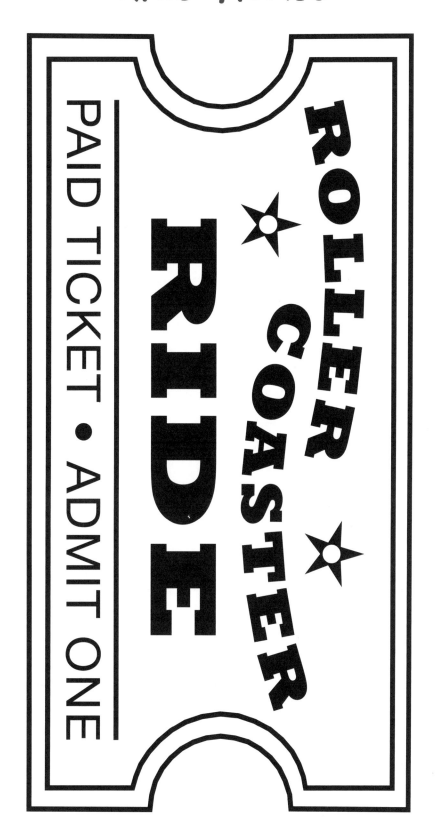

ROLLER COASTER RIDE

PAID TICKET • ADMIT ONE

Heaven Gift Box

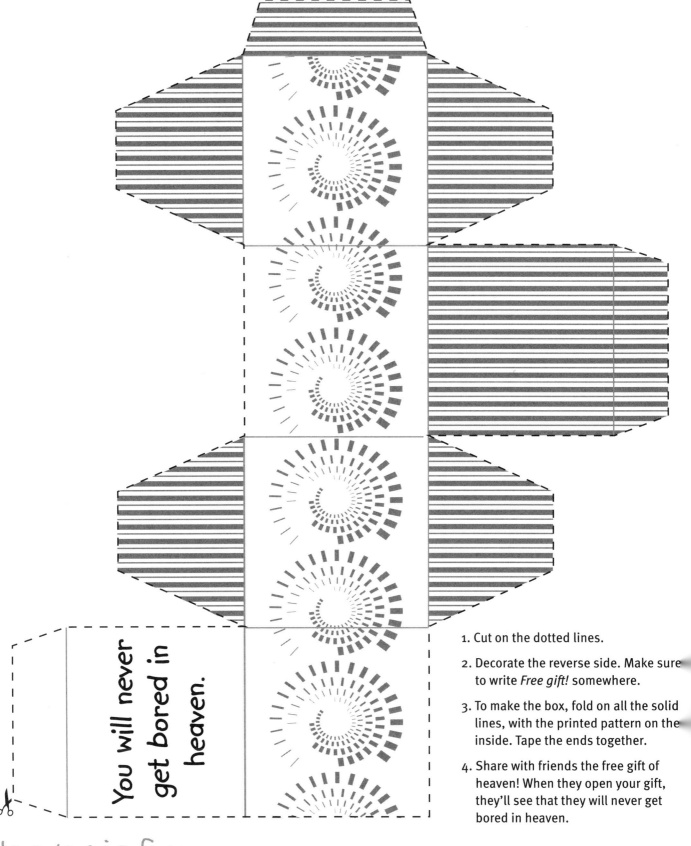

You will never get bored in heaven.

1. Cut on the dotted lines.

2. Decorate the reverse side. Make sure to write *Free gift!* somewhere.

3. To make the box, fold on all the solid lines, with the printed pattern on the inside. Tape the ends together.

4. Share with friends the free gift of heaven! When they open your gift, they'll see that they will never get bored in heaven.

Heaven is for **Real** for kids

64

The Angel's Sword Is Covered in Flames and Is Really Powerful

Making It Real

Kids will discover that  *the angel's sword is covered in flames and is really powerful.*

Objectives

Kids will:

✔ Learn that they have strong and powerful angels protecting them.

✔ Talk about things they need protection from.

✔ Create their own swords as a reminder that angels protect them.

You'll need...

☐ several Bibles

☐ several large pieces of poster board, cut into notebook-size pieces

☐ several pairs of scissors

☐ 1 copy of the "Angel's Sword" handout (p. 73) per child, plus a few extras

☐ aluminum foil

☐ red and orange tissue paper

☐ pencils

☐ tape

What the Bible Says

Matthew 18:10

Matthew 18:10 tells us that children are so valuable and precious that God has angels in heaven to protect them. Colton Burpo was amazed by the size and power of the angels he saw in heaven. And these angels were everywhere. Colton said that the angel Michael's sword was "as big as Dad!" Colton says this sword is covered in flames and is really powerful.

Jesus warned people not to look down on children. Yet we still tend to do so today, even when our cultures and societies value and protect kids more than any time in history. We often see kids as an annoyance or disturbance. We brush them away and tell them we're too busy. But Jesus knows how important children are and how valuable they are to the kingdom of heaven. Jesus said that children's angels are always in the presence of God.

There are numerous Scriptures confirming that angels are big, strong, and powerful. In Matthew 28:2-4, we get to see one in action: "At that time there was a strong earthquake. An angel of the Lord came down from heaven. The angel went to the tomb and rolled the stone away from the entrance. Then he sat on the stone. He was shining as bright as lightning. His clothes were white as snow. The soldiers guarding the tomb were very frightened of the angel. They shook with fear and then became like dead men."

Revelation 12:7 says, "Then there was a war in heaven. Michael and his angels fought against the dragon. The dragon and his angels fought back." When Colton visited heaven, he saw Michael as the biggest angel and noticed that *his sword is covered in flames and is really powerful.*

It's comforting for kids—who can all relate to how it feels to be afraid, sad, confused, or hurt—to know that God gives these mighty and powerful angels to protect us.

Kids often tend to think of angels as fairylike creatures—not the mighty and powerful beings they really are. Movies and television don't help this misconception when angels are portrayed as humans with wings who are good, but not so powerful. Angels are sometimes portrayed as ghostly and ethereal, floating leisurely through the air. Kids might even think that they'll become angels when they die. (If Colton's memories are correct, we'll get wings like angels. But, we will not become angels.)

There are many misconceptions kids have when it comes to angels, but this lesson will help kids understand how they're so important to God that his mighty and amazing, powerful angels are watching over them. It will be important that you help kids understand that, like heaven, we might not see angels, but they're around. In this lesson, your kids will learn that: *the angel's sword is covered in flames and is really powerful.*

The Lesson

Let's Get Real

Help, Help Me, Angel!

Welcome kids warmly. Then to start the lesson tell them you'll be talking about things that scare you. Share an age-appropriate situation that scared you and what happened. Have kids close their eyes for a moment and think about something that makes them scared. Give kids 30 seconds to think, and then ask for kids to tell about what scares them. Allow time for many kids to share.

Say: **We all have things that scare us—but I'm going to let you in on an important secret today. We have special helpers who protect us: angels! And angels do many things, including protecting us and helping us feel safe. In fact, one angel we'll talk about is named Michael. Michael is really tall and** 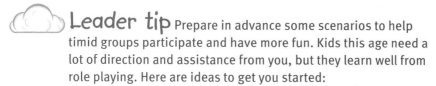 *his sword is covered in flames and is really powerful.* **Let's see what Michael might do about some of those scary things you shared— and we'll see how this powerful, mighty angel might be here to help you and protect you.**

Have kids form groups of four or five. Join in if there's a smaller group. Have groups plan to act out a scenario where God might send an angel like Michael to help. The group will then act out its scenario with each person taking a role. For example, if someone is afraid of bullies at school, a couple of kids from the group can pretend to be the bullies, the child who shared will be herself, and another child can be Michael. When the "bullies" start to pick on the child, "Michael" can stand in front of her and tell her to run, then tell the others to go away.

Leader tip Prepare in advance some scenarios to help timid groups participate and have more fun. Kids this age need a lot of direction and assistance from you, but they learn well from role playing. Here are ideas to get you started:

- being bullied on the bus
- being afraid of the dark at bedtime
- learning how to do something new and scary (like ride a bike)
- going to summer camp for the first time

After each group acts out its scenario, have kids discuss with their groups:

- **Why do you think God has angels to protect us?**

- **What's one thing you'd like God to send an angel like Michael to help you with?**

Allow two minutes. Alert kids when there are 30 seconds left. When time is up, have kids turn their attention back to you. Then ask willing kids to share their answers to the last question with the entire group.

Say: **God's angels aren't wimpy. They're strong! Let's dig into what the Bible has to say about God's angels.**

Making the Bible Real

Michael's Sword Is Really Powerful! (Matthew 18:10)

Say: **Angels are real, and God has sent them to protect us, especially kids. Remember that God loves kids, and he wants to make sure the angels protect you.**

The Bible tells us in Matthew 18:1-4 about a time the disciples came to Jesus with a question. Distribute Bibles, and have kids form pairs. Pair readers with nonreaders, as necessary. If you have an uneven number of children, join in so every child has a partner.

When kids have finished reading, discuss the passage as a group.

Ask: • **What do you think it means to be "humble like a child"?**

• **What was it like to hear that Jesus said children are the greatest in heaven?**

• **Why do you think children might be the greatest in heaven?**

Say: **Each of you is very important to God. The Bible says Jesus loves you all so much! Jesus explained to the disciples that unless people "turned away from sin" and stopped doing wrong things and instead became like children, they'd never get into heaven. But he said if someone becomes humble like a little child, that person will become the greatest in heaven.**

Have kids stand and face away from you.

Say: **Silently think about something you did recently that you know was wrong. Maybe it's not cleaning your room when your parents told you to, not doing something your teacher asked you to do, or calling someone a mean name. It could be lots of things. Now when you think of that thing, pretend to hold it in your hand.** Pause. **Make a tight fist around that bad thing, and throw it as hard as you can against the wall.** Pause. **Once you've thrown it, turn around and face me.**

Heaven is for
Real
for kids

"Turning away" from sin means you know what you've done is wrong and you turn away from it and try not to do it again.

Jesus said people need to become like little children to get into the kingdom of heaven. That's partly because when kids mess up, they turn to their parents. Jesus also wants us to turn to him when we mess up.

Let's read on to see what Jesus says about kids and angels.

Have partners read Matthew 18:10. Then read the following questions out loud, allowing a minute in between each for partners to discuss.

- **How would you describe angels to someone who didn't know about them?**

- **The next time you feel scared, how will you remember that God has angels watching out for you?**

Ask willing kids to share their answers to the last question with the entire group.

Say: Jesus warned people not to look down on kids because they are precious to God and they have angels watching over them, just like the angel Michael, whose 🖉 *sword is covered in flames and is really powerful.*

Real-Life Application

Powerful Swords

Remind kids of Colton's story. Tell kids that Colton said he was amazed by the size and power of the angels he saw in heaven and how they were all around.

Say: **Colton said that the angel Michael's sword was "as big as Dad!" Colton says  *his sword is covered in flames and is really powerful.***

Have kids show you how big they think the angels watching over them are by standing up and making themselves look as big as they can. Explain that the Bible also tells about angels, and a sword of fire that flashes. Have partners open their Bibles to Genesis 3:24. Ask a willing child to read about angels guarding the Garden of Eden alongside a sword of fire "that flashed around in every direction."

Say: **Today we're going to make a pretend sword that you can keep in your room to remind you that angels are protecting you, just like the angel Michael, whose *sword is covered in flames and is really powerful.***

Leader tip Boys especially love hearing about Michael. If you have time, go deeper into the Bible to find more stories about Michael. In Revelation 12:7, Michael fights a dragon. In Daniel 10:13, Michael comes to earth to lend a helping hand. According to Colton's story, Michael is around 12 feet tall. Help kids picture this by grabbing a ladder and marking on a tree how tall he would be standing outside your church.

Have kids sit at a table or on the floor. Kids will each need a copy of the "Angel's Sword" handout (p. 73), a piece of poster board, scissors, a pencil, and enough aluminum foil to cover the sword. They'll also need red and orange tissue paper to tape onto the sword to look like flames. If you have younger kids who struggle with scissors, cut the poster board into sword shapes beforehand.

Allow time for kids to cut their swords out of poster board, using the handout as a template. Have older kids help younger kids as needed. Show kids how to cover their swords with foil so they appear shiny. Then help kids tape strips of red and orange tissue paper to the blades of their swords to represent flames.

After kids have finished, have them hold their swords high in the air.

Say: **Take this special sword home as a reminder that you have angels protecting you always. Remember what Colton said about Michael when he saw this great angel in heaven: *His sword is covered in flames and is really powerful.***

Prepare a sample sword ahead of time to show kids what they're making. Make your sword simple so kids feel confident they can make one, too.

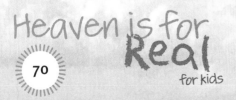

Real-Life Commitment

Share Your Fears

Say: Knowing there are angels protecting us can give us courage! It can help us know we don't have to be afraid. Let's practice with our swords.

Have kids form new pairs. If you have an uneven number of children, join in so every child has a partner. Have kids hold their swords. Tell kids to take turns pretending to be an angel sent by God to protect their partner. One partner should say things he or she is afraid of; then the other partner can pretend to be an angel, holding a sword up high and saying, "God's angels can protect you by…" and explaining one way God's angels can help.

Allow four minutes. When there are two minutes left, tell kids to swap roles. When time is up, have kids turn their attention back to you.

Say: God sees all of his children as valuable. It's amazing that he has angels to protect us. Those angels are strong and powerful, like Michael, whose *sword is covered in flames and is really powerful.*

Colton's Challenge

Closing Prayer

Gather kids for a closing prayer.

Say: Turn to your partner again. Let's pray for each other to remember that you're each so valuable to God that he has angels watching over you. Remember that those angels will protect you, so you don't need to be afraid. I'm about to pray. When I come to the part where I ask God to help our friends, I want you to say out loud the name of your partner. Let's pray.

Pray: Dear Jesus, today we've learned that you have angels watching over us, like Michael, who has *a sword that is covered in flames and is really powerful.* Thank you for those angels who keep us safe so we never need to be afraid. Please help our friends...(give time for kids to say names). Remember that they're valuable to God, and that's why he has angels watch over them. In your name, amen.

Remind kids that when they start to feel afraid, they can look at their swords and remember that God has angels to protect them.

Angel's Sword

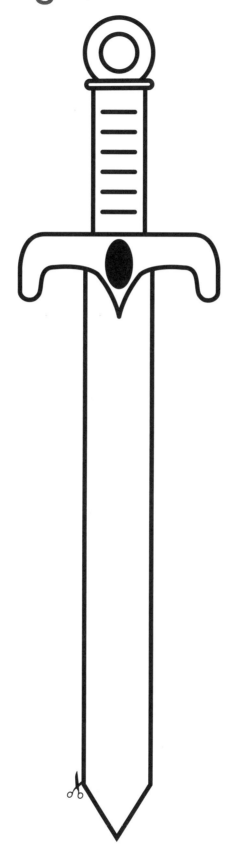

In Heaven, All Animals Get Along

Making It Real

Kids will discover that ✏ *in heaven, all animals get along.*

Objectives

Kids will:

- ✔ Discover that animals and people all get along in heaven.
- ✔ Create animal masks and act out how animals might treat each other in heaven.
- ✔ Think about people who don't get along now but will in heaven.
- ✔ Explore how being like Jesus can help them get along with their enemies.

You'll need...

- ☐ several Bibles
- ☐ paper
- ☐ hat or bowl
- ☐ round paper plates
- ☐ chenille craft wires
- ☐ yarn
- ☐ cotton balls
- ☐ washable markers and crayons
- ☐ several pairs of scissors
- ☐ tape and glue sticks
- ☐ soft instrumental music and CD player

What the Bible Says

 Isaiah 11:6

Colton Burpo not only saw people and angels in heaven, but he also saw animals in heaven. During his time there, he noticed that all the animals got along with each other. Isaiah 11:6 says: "Then wolves will live in peace with lambs. And leopards will lie down to rest with goats. Calves, lions, and young bulls will eat together. And a little child will lead them."

It's amazing to think that animals that are such great enemies here on earth live peacefully with one another in heaven. Here on earth, animals and humans often fight with each other. But because of God's amazing grace, there'll be no fighting between friends, animals, or humans. Proverbs 16:7 says: "A person should live so that he pleases the Lord. If he does, even his enemies will make peace with him." When we're in heaven, we'll all be at peace with one another.

Chapter 11 of Isaiah talks about the restoration of Jesus' kingdom. Hosea 2:18 refers again to this restoration when it says, "At that time I will make an agreement for them. It will be with the wild animals, the birds and the crawling things. I will remove from the land the bow and the sword and the weapons of war. Then my people will live in safety." God plans for us to have a relationship with him, enter into peace, and rest in heaven.

If you ask most kids about what kinds of things they think they'll encounter in heaven, there's a good chance they'll wonder about animals—especially favorite pets they've lost. Kids love animals, and explaining to your kids that animals will be in heaven helps make the concept of heaven all the more real to them. One aspect that's confusing to kids is how natural enemies such as wolves and lambs could be together and how a lion could lie down with a baby goat. They might wonder about how these supposed animal enemies could be friendly. This lesson will help kids understand that even earthly enemies get along in heaven. Not just animals, but people, too. In this lesson, your kids will learn that ✎ *in heaven, all animals get along.*

The Lesson

Let's Get Real

It's a Circus!

Have kids sit at a table. Ask them to think of an animal and shout out its name. Once kids have responded, ask them to shout out the name of that animal's natural enemy. Explain to them that, for example, if they shouted a lion, maybe its natural enemy would be an elephant.

Let kids shout out animal names, and then tell them they're going to have fun pretending to *be* those animals—but they have to look the part. They'll need to make masks to represent an animal.

Explain that kids will draw an animal name out of the hat or bowl you prepared earlier and then make a mask representing that animal. Help younger kids read the animal name they chose. Have lots of craft supplies available for kids to choose from to help create their masks. Explain how they can use the chenille craft wires to make whiskers, the cotton balls to make fur, and markers or crayons to color their animals. Some kids may need help cutting out eye holes with the scissors. The masks don't have to be perfect; they simply represent the animals kids selected. Make sure kids put their names on the inside of the masks. When kids are done decorating, ask them to hold their masks in front of their faces.

Have kids form a circle. Explain to kids that you want them to move around the room and act like the animal on each of their masks. If they come across other animals that are the enemy of their animals, they can chase them, growl at them, or roar at them. Make sure kids know that physical contact like hitting or tagging isn't allowed. You room will soon be filled with dogs chasing cats, lions roaring at lambs, mice chasing elephants, and bears growling at everybody!

Allow three minutes. Alert kids when there are 30 seconds left. When time is up, have kids turn their attention back to you. Then have them form a circle on the floor. As they sit down, tell them to find a place next to a person they just chased or growled at.

Say: **The Bible says there'll be animals in heaven. And here's the amazing part:** 🖉 ***In heaven, all animals get along.***

Write the names of various common animals on slips of paper, and put them in a hat or bowl. You'll need one animal per child, plus a few extras. Set out these supplies: round paper plates, chenille craft wires, yarn, cotton balls, markers, scissors, and glue or glue sticks.

Making the Bible Real

In Heaven, All Animals Get Along (Isaiah 11:6)

Say: **Animals may fight here on earth, but there are animals in heaven, too, and they get along just fine.** Have kids form pairs with readers helping nonreaders. Distribute Bibles to each pair and ask them to find Isaiah 11:6. Ask a willing child to read the verse. Instruct the reader to pause at the name of each animal, and let the rest of the class make the noise that animal makes.

Say: **Now let's act like this verse tells us animals act in heaven. Remember that** 🖉 *in heaven, all animals get along.* **We might see mice giving elephants high fives, or lions hugging zebras, or cats and dogs playing together. Ready? Go!**

> **Leader tip** Talking donkeys, Noah's ark, the very big fish that swallowed Jonah...the Bible is full of animals. Colton remembers being able to play with elephants, kangaroos, and even lions in heaven. Kids might wonder how it can be safe to be around lions, but remind them of Daniel (chapter 6) and how he survived the lion's den, thanks to God.

Have kids pretend to be animals again, except this time they'll be nice to each other. Praise any animals being peaceful together that normally wouldn't be friends in the wild. Help guide this activity by encouraging cooperation between different animals.

Allow three minutes. Alert kids when there are 30 seconds left. When time is up, have kids turn their attention back to you and sit in a circle.

Ask: • **Why don't all animals get along on earth?**

• **Why do you think animals get along in heaven?**

Say: **Not only will all animals get along with each other, but all people will, too! Let's talk about that some more.**

Real-Life Application

Acting Like Animals

Say: **When someone is misbehaving or doing wrong, sometimes people say that person is "acting like an animal." And just like animals fight with each other, people can hurt other people. It may not be with claws or by biting, but people can hurt others with the words they say.**

Gather the kids' animal masks, but let them know you'll give them back soon. **Today, we're going to pretend animals can talk. I'm going to hold up one of your animal masks, and I want you to pretend to pick on that animal. For instance, if I held up an elephant, you might say, "You have big ears!" or "Your nose is huge!"**

Leader tip Throughout the activities, have older kids pair up with younger ones. The older kids can help their younger friends who may not yet be reading, or who may need help understanding certain questions.

Hold up the masks, one by one, and let the kids come up with things to say for each animal.

Have kids form pairs. If you have an uneven number of children, join in so every child has a partner. Read the following questions out loud, one at a time, allowing a minute in between questions for partners to discuss.

- **Tell about a time you saw people say hurtful things to one another.**

- **How is making fun of people like or unlike making fun of animals for how they look or act?**

- **What's a good way to handle it if you see someone saying hurtful things to another person?**

Ask willing kids to share their answers to the last question with the entire group.

Say: **Just like how 🖉 *in heaven, all animals get along*, we should try our best to get along with each other here on earth.**

Real-Life Commitment

Be a Real Friend

Have kids sit in a circle, and give back the animal masks they made.

Say: Sadly, there are people in our world who are enemies, just like how your pretend animals were enemies. **Hold up your masks and make animal sounds like your animal would make.** Give kids time to make their animal noises. **Animals growl to show anger. Growl and show me what your animal would sound like when it's angry.** Let kids give you a hearty growl.

Ask: • But what do people say and do to show anger?

• Why do you think people get mad at each other?

Say: People get mad at each other and become enemies for lots of reasons—and they always have. Even back in the Bible times, people had enemies. Let's hear about some of those people. Hold up a Bible and remind kids that this story, like everything else in the Bible, is true.

Have kids form new pairs. If you have an uneven number of children, join in so every child has a partner.

☁ **Leader tip** You may want to explain to kids that the following stories can be found in 1 Samuel.

Say: Saul was a king who had a son named Jonathan. Jonathan was next in line to be king. But Saul disobeyed God, so God chose another boy—named David—to be the next king, instead of Saul's son Jonathan. Ouch, right?

Ask: • How do you think Jonathan felt about David, the boy who would be the next king instead of him?

• Tell about a time you or someone you know felt jealous.

Allow time for kids to discuss with their partners.

Say: Jonathan knew David was going to be the next king, but rather than being mad, he chose to become David's friend. Jonathan even helped David escape once when Saul tried to kill him! When Jonathan realized his father, Saul, would keep trying to kill David, he asked Saul why—and Saul got really mad at Jonathan.

Ask:
- **How do you think Jonathan handled this situation? How about Saul, his dad?**

- **What are ways you've helped people become friends or forgive each other?**

- **How was this story like or unlike what relationships are like in heaven?**

Discuss with the entire group.

Say: Just as 🖉 *all animals get along in heaven,* people will get along in heaven, too!

Say: **When Colton was in heaven, he saw how all the animals were peaceful and happy with each other. We know that people will get along in heaven just as the animals do. But we can also get along with people today, before we get to heaven. Jesus is such a great example of how to be a good friend. He loves everybody, no matter what. He always forgives people and gives them hope.** Read the following questions out loud, allowing a minute in between each for partners to discuss.

- **Why would you choose to be someone's friend rather than enemy?**

- **How can you be a good friend like Jesus?**

Ask willing kids to share their answers to the last question with the entire group.

Say: **Because Jesus sets such a good example for us, we can follow him and be that kind of friend now, even before we get to heaven. When we choose to be good friends, we can get along with others just like** 🖉 *in heaven, where all animals get along.*

Colton's Challenge

Closing Prayer

Gather kids for a closing prayer. Explain that this week they will pray in the form of a letter to God. Give kids each a sheet of paper and a marker or crayon. Play some soft instrumental music as kids write their letters. Tell kids that the words do not have to be spelled the right way because God knows what's in their hearts. If you have younger kids who can't write, tell them to draw pictures instead.

Prompt kids to start by telling them to thank God for helping them learn that *in heaven, all animals get along.* Have kids ask God to help them remember ways to be a friend this week. Kids can keep their letters to God to remind them that Jesus is a perfect example of how to be a friend, and we can follow his example of love and forgiveness in our friendships.

In Heaven, You Live Forever With God

Making It Real

Kids will discover that  *in heaven, you live forever with God.*

Objectives

Kids will:

✔ Talk about the adventures they hope to have in life.

✔ Draw pictures showing John's vision of heaven.

✔ Understand that life with God the Father on earth is practice for life with God the Father in heaven.

✔ Plan ways to share God's good news this week.

You'll need...

☐ several Bibles

☐ paper

☐ many bright crayons, plus 1 black crayon per child

☐ toothpicks

☐ craft supplies such as large sheets of paper, construction paper, magazines or newspapers, tape or glue, chenille craft wires, markers, and modeling clay

☐ praise music CD and a CD player

☐ a variety of toys for the activity on p. 85

What the Bible Says

📖 *Revelation 21:3-4*

Although Colton's visit to heaven was a short one, he knows he'll be back some-day to stay forever. Until he goes back, though, Colton tells people he sees about Jesus and what he saw in heaven. In some ways Colton is like John, one of Jesus' disciples. After Jesus died and rose again, John became a pastor. He wrote the Gospel of John as well as 1, 2, and 3 John. Today we sometimes refer to John as "the love pastor" for his emphasis on the great love of God (for examples, see John 3:16 or 1 John 4:7-8). John was arrested and exiled to the Greek island of

Patmos for preaching the good news about Jesus. While he was there, God gave John a vision that included scenes of what heaven is like. Then John wrote the book of Revelation. According to John's vision, someone sitting on a throne proclaimed that God's home is with his people and that death, sorrow, tears, and pain will all be gone forever. Now that's a place we can look forward to!

In heaven there'll be no more tears or pain, but there sure is plenty of both on earth. Yet if we got serious about following God's instructions, there could be less sorrow and more joy in this world. Psalm 19 simply points out that God's laws are perfect, trustworthy, right, pure, and true; following them will revive the soul, make the simple wise, and bring joy and insight for living.

In 1 Chronicles 16:23-24, 34, we see ways to thank God for the blessing of heaven: "Sing to the Lord, all the earth. Every day tell how he saves us. Tell the nations about the Lord's glory. Tell all peoples about his wonderful works... Thank the Lord because he is good. His love continues forever."

It's true: God's faithful love continues forever—here on earth and all the way to eternity in heaven—hallelujah! God's people have the responsibility and joy to proclaim God's good news on earth so that others can have a relationship with him and live forever in heaven with our good and loving God.

From Kids' Point of View

Kids this age are developing a sense of time. Do you remember as a child anticipating Christmas morning? Or how summer days seemed to last an eternity? Or how someone at an age that seems young to you now seemed ancient to you then? To young kids, life holds infinite opportunities, and they unconsciously expect that their lives on earth will last forever.

But they may also have a growing awareness of death. Perhaps a pet, neighbor, or loved one has died. What then? What happens after death? In children's media, when cartoon characters flatten and pop back into shape as if nothing happened, death is entertainment; in life, death is unknowable and can be creepy.

You will disperse the gloom and help kids begin to grasp some amazingly good news. In this lesson, kids will learn that 🖉 *in heaven, you live forever with God.*

The Lesson

Let's Get Real

Adventure Time

Have kids gather in the center of your room. Tell them to find an object in the room to represent something they want to do in life. It can be something they want to become or someplace they want to go. For example, a child could choose blocks to show that he or she wants to be a builder who builds skyscrapers, or a toy car to represent taking a trip across the country.

When everyone has found an object, have kids form pairs. If you have an uneven number of children, join in so every child has a partner. Have partners discuss why they chose their objects.

Allow two minutes. Alert kids when there are 30 seconds left. When time is up, have kids turn their attention back to you. Then ask willing kids to share their objects with the entire group.

Once everyone who wants to share has had a chance to, tell kids that there is not enough time to be able to do everything that was said, because our time is limited.

Say: **People only get so many years to live on earth, so the adventures we get to live here are limited by that time. But** *in heaven, you live forever with God.* **You can have countless adventures in heaven, all while praising our good God!** Read the following questions out loud, one at a time, allowing a minute in between questions for partners to discuss.

- **Tell about a time you wanted to do something, but you had to wait a long time to do it, like opening Christmas gifts.**

- **Imagine a circle. Find the end. Just like a circle is endless and goes on and on, so will our time with God. How would you explain to a friend what "forever" means?**

- **What's something you're looking forward to with all the time you'll have in heaven?**

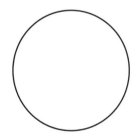

Making the Bible Real

In Heaven, You Live Forever With God (Revelation 21:3-4)

Get Ready

You'll need lots of bright crayons for kids to share. For each child, you'll need a sheet of paper, a black crayon, and a toothpick.

You may want to have kids work at a table so they are able to press down while they're drawing.

Distribute paper and crayons. Tell kids to color one side of their paper. Don't have them draw anything in particular, just have them color the entire page randomly with bright, vibrant colors. Encourage them to use every color but black; they will use that color in the next step. As they color, pause every now and then and tell kids to show each other a happy face, a scared face, an excited face, a sick face, a hurt face, and a sad face. Ask willing kids to tell about a time when they got sick, hurt, or felt really sad.

When everyone is done coloring, tell kids that they will now color over their art with the black crayon. Tell them to press down hard and cover up all the color.

Say: **When Jesus lived on earth, he had crowds of people who followed him, listening to him and learning from him. One of Jesus' followers was John. After Jesus died and came back to life again to be with God in heaven, John became a pastor who taught others how much Jesus loves us. One time God gave John a vision of what heaven will be like. A vision is sort of like a dream, except John was wide awake.**

When kids are finished coloring, say: **Close your eyes and listen as I read just a little bit of John's vision to you. Try to see in your mind what John tells us about heaven. When I've read it once, I'll tell you to open your eyes and you can draw what John described.**

Ask kids to close their eyes as you read Revelation 21:3-4 slowly and with emphasis.

Ask kids to open their eyes, and give them each a toothpick. By scratching off the black, they can make a bright design. Have kids draw what they heard John describe. As they draw, read the passage another two or three times.

Allow five minutes, and give a 30-second warning. When time is up, have kids turn their attention back to you. Ask for volunteers to show their artwork to the group. Then read the following questions one at a time, allowing time in between for discussion.

Ask:
- **What do you think life would be like if there was no more death, sadness, crying, or pain?**

- **What does it mean to you that God will make his home with us and we will never have a reason to cry ever again?**

- **In a scary situation, how does it feel to have parents nearby? God is the biggest parent ever. What will it feel like always having him around?**

Say: 📝 *In heaven, you live forever with God.* **God will be at home with us just as our families are at home together, except it'll be even better because we won't get hurt or be sad or cry ever again. Colton Burpo experienced this during his time in heaven. His body was very sick and he felt terrible—he was dying. But when he visited heaven, he forgot all about how sick he was. He had a great time, in fact! He was happy, safe, and healthy—nothing like what his body on earth felt like.**

Real-Life Application

"A Full Life"

Say: **Life in heaven is going to be great, but God also wants us to have a great life now.** Have a willing child look up and read John 10:10. **One of the best ways to have a great life on earth is to follow God's instructions.** Hold up your Bible. **And in the Bible it tells us how to live for God. Let's read Psalm 19:7-9 and make up some motions to help us remember.**

Before you continue, ask a willing child to describe what "orders" are. Ask someone else about the words "commands" or "commandments." Finally, ask kids if anyone knows the word "judgments." Be ready to explain the words in case you have a group that's unfamiliar with the words.

Say: *Orders*, *commands* **and** *commandments*, **and** *judgments* **are all words that describe the same idea: They're all about the way God wants us to live. And living God's way is always the best idea.**

Tell kids they're going to make up body motions to go with Psalm 19:7-9 to help them remember what it says. Have everyone stand.

Say: **"The Lord's teachings are perfect. They give new strength."** Explain to kids that line means when we follow God's rules, we get stronger on the inside. Have kids come up with ways to show strength.

Say: **"The Lord's rules can be trusted. They make plain people wise."** Explain to kids that this line means we should trust God and follow his will, and we will make smarter choices. Have kids come up with a way to show wisdom or good choices.

Say: **"The Lord's orders are right. They make people happy."** Remind kids that when we follow God's laws, we'll have joy in our lives. Have kids come up with new motions to show happiness.

Say: "The Lord's commandments are pure. They light up the way." Tell kids that God's rules are like having a flashlight in a dark place. Have kids make up a new motion to remember this verse.

Say: "It is good to respect the Lord. That respect will last forever." Tell kids that in heaven, we can love God forever. Have kids make up a motion that shows respect.

Say: "The Lord's judgments are true. They are completely right." Remind kids that God is real, fair, and loving. Have kids make up one last motion.

When you've got six motions, practice them again as you repeat the passage.

Ask: • How can we show our respect to God?

• What can we do when it feels hard to respect and follow God's rules?

Ask for willing kids to share their answers with the entire group.

Say: *In heaven, you live forever with God.* And we can experience a little bit of heaven when we live for God here on earth. Living this way also saves us from some of the pain that comes through sin, which is disobeying God's perfect commands.

Real-Life Commitment

Good News

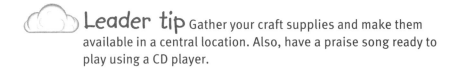 Leader tip Gather your craft supplies and make them available in a central location. Also, have a praise song ready to play using a CD player.

Say: **Let's take a moment to think about how great God is. Not only does he want us to live forever with him in heaven, but he also takes good care of us while we're practicing to live with him here on earth.**

Have kids form pairs, pairing readers with nonreaders. If you have an uneven number of children, join in so every child has a partner.

Say: **Tell your partner about great things God's done in your life. Then come up with one creative way to share those things with all of us. You might sing, create a poster, act it out, come up with more body motions, make a sculpture, or whatever you want to do to praise God.**

Play the praise song as pairs work on their presentations. When the song is finished, have pairs present for one another. When all pairs have presented, lead kids in a round of applause for God.

Distribute Bibles and have pairs look up 1 Chronicles 16:23-24, 34. Ask a willing child to read the passage, pausing after each sentence while the rest of the kids give a cheer for God.

Say: **Because God does so many great things and because we want to live with God now on earth and forever in heaven, we can sing of his goodness and proclaim his good news to the entire world.** 🖉 *In heaven, you live forever with God.* **That's good news for us, and good news we can share with others who don't yet know Jesus.**

Colton's Challenge

Closing Prayer

Gather kids for a closing prayer. Explain that this prayer time will be personal, and just between them and God. Ask kids to pray silently after you reread 1 Chronicles 16:23-24, 34. Then wrap up the prayer time with a group prayer.

Pray: **Dear Jesus, today we've learned that** ***in heaven, we will live forever with you.* Help us remember to follow your instructions. Please help us remember to shout out praise to you for what you are doing for us. And help us be loud with our praise; others need to hear how good you are. In your name, amen.**

The Holy Spirit Helps You When You Pray

Making It Real

Kids will discover that  *the Holy Spirit helps you when you pray.*

Objectives

Kids will:

- ✔ Try to communicate without words.
- ✔ Imagine God's throne room.
- ✔ Use their bodies to create a throne.
- ✔ Consider how a balloon is like the Holy Spirit.
- ☐ Discover how to pray boldly.
- ☐ Choose a time to spend with God in prayer every day.

You'll need...

- ☐ several Bibles
- ☐ 1 copy of the "Three Simple Tasks" handout (p. 99) per 2 kids, plus extra copies
- ☐ digital camera (optional)
- ☐ 1 balloon per child (do not inflate)

What the Bible Says

📖 *Hebrews 4:16*

During Colton's trip to heaven, he was invited into the throne room. Hebrews 4:16 says, "Let us, then, feel free to come before God's throne. Here there is grace. And we can receive mercy and grace to help us when we need it."

The fourth chapter of Hebrews highlights God's promise of heaven for those who trust Jesus. The writer laments that people fall away from faith, and he presses his readers to hold firm to their beliefs. People are weak, but God shines through our weakness if we let him. Jesus sits in heaven, inviting us to come boldly into his throne room in search of his mercy and grace.

In Psalm 99:1, we read that "The Lord is king. Let the nations shake with fear. He sits between the gold creatures with wings. Let the earth shake." It demands that we acknowledge the awe- and worship-inspiring kingship of our God. Nations tremble and the entire earth quakes, while we both exalt God and bow low before his feet. God is holy and we owe him respect and honor. We humbly seek God with reverence.

While in the throne room, Colton experienced the Holy Spirit. While Jesus can be simple to understand, the Holy Spirit can be more difficult to comprehend. Acts 1:8 promises that we will receive the Holy Spirit's power to be God's witnesses wherever we go. Romans 5:5 says the Holy Spirit fills our hearts with God's love so that we can know how dearly God loves us. And Romans 8:26-27 assures us that the Spirit helps us in our weaknesses, particularly when we don't know what to pray. The Spirit will actually pray for us, pleading on our behalf and in harmony with God's will.

From Kids' Point of View

Prayer can be a difficult concept to grasp for some kids. Some might not understand that prayer is an opportunity to talk with God, the one who created them and loves them so much. Sometimes kids may feel a little intimidated by praying. They hear adults pray and think they must use fancy language or say certain things. And some of your kids might think that prayer only counts if they close their eyes and bow their heads. Throughout this lesson, kids will learn that prayer can happen anywhere, and they will see that praying is an amazing way to get closer to God.

In this lesson, your kids will learn that ✐ *the Holy Spirit helps you when you pray.*

The Lesson

Let's Get Real

No Talking

Have kids form pairs. If you have an uneven number of children, join in so every child has a partner.

Tell kids they're about to play a game. Have kids separate, with one partner standing on one side of the room and the other partner standing directly across the room. Give each child on one side of the room a copy of the "Three Simple Tasks" handout.

> **Leader tip** This activity requires reading by half the kids. Encourage readers to pair with nonreaders, and guide each to the appropriate side of the room. Assist as needed.

Say: **The challenge for you all is to get your partner to complete the three simple tasks listed on the paper. Without saying what the tasks are, do you think you can get your partner to do these things?** Let kids weigh in. Then turn to the other side of the room and say: **When I say "go," look to your partner for instruction and try to do what's on the list. Ready, set... Wait! There's one more thing.** Look at the kids with the list. **You all can't say anything. Not one word. OK, ready? Go!**

Allow three minutes. Alert kids when there are two minutes left, and one minute left. When time is up, read the following questions out loud, one at a time, allowing a minute in between questions for partners to discuss.

- **Describe what it was like to get your partner to do the tasks.**

- **What would've helped you in this experience?**

- **How is this like or unlike trying to get God to do something for you?**

Ask willing kids to share their answers to the last question with the entire group.

Say: **God loves us and wants us to talk with him. That's what prayer is— talking to and listening to God. Sometimes we feel like we don't know what to pray—or how to pray. But the good news is that** ✎ *the Holy Spirit helps you when you pray.*

Make one copy of the "Three Simple Tasks" handout (p. 99) for every two kids.

Making the Bible Real

The Holy Spirit Helps You When You Pray (Hebrews 4:16)

You'll need a big, open space where kids can create "chairs" with their bodies. If you can't move furniture aside, consider taking kids to another room or a patch of lawn if you have easy access.

Form two groups.

Say: **In the throne room in heaven, Colton says he saw a huge chair fit for a king and little chairs for kids. Use your bodies to make a big, fancy chair for someone in your group.**

Encourage kids to work together to "build" a throne using only their bodies. When they're done, tell kids to hold their positions. Then point out each "chair" and applaud kids' efforts.

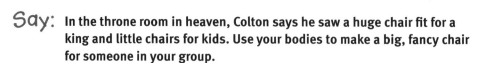 Leader tip This activity might make for a great photo opportunity. Take a picture of each "chair," then later print the pictures and make a poster to hang in your meeting space. Include the Bible point: *The Holy Spirit helps you when you pray.* Kids like to see pictures of themselves and their friends having fun, and it will be a visual reminder of what they've learned today.

Ask: • **What qualifies someone to have such a special seat?**

• **Why do people bow before royal people like kings and queens?**

Ask for willing kids to share responses to the last question with the entire group.

Say: **Maybe you've read fairy tales where a regular person kneels before the king to make a special request. But the stories in the Bible are all true. And bowing is a sign of respect.** Distribute Bibles, and help kids find Hebrews 4:16. Ask kids to kneel as they read the verse out loud together, with older kids helping younger ones.

God sits on a great big throne in heaven, and he deserves our respect. Let's bow down low as if we're bowing before God the Father's heavenly throne. Pause while kids bow. **While I read this passage from Psalm 99, continue to bow and imagine yourself bowing before God.**

Read Psalm 99:1, 5 with drama and solemnity. Then pause for 20 seconds.

Invite kids to sit up.

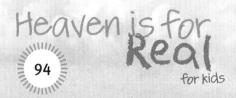

Say: Jesus and the Holy Spirit are in God's throne room, too. Jesus died on the cross to save us from our sins. God's Holy Spirit is here with us when we need help.

Ask kids to think of a way that someone might need help. Ask willing kids to pose in a way that shows the person needing help. Give kids a chance to guess what kind of situation each scene portrays. Then invite new kids to come up and pose.

Have kids form three groups. Give each group one of the following verses to look up: Acts 1:8, Romans 5:5, and Romans 8:26-27. Have one person from each group read the verse(s) out loud to their small group. Ask kids to listen for the kinds of help the Holy Spirit gives us. Then ask a willing child from each group to read the group's verse(s) out loud to the rest of the groups. Whenever kids hear a way the Holy Spirit helps them, they can stand up and then sit back down.

After all the verses are read, read the following questions out loud, allowing allowing a minute in between each for groups to discuss.

- **When do you think you could use the Holy Spirit's help this week?**

- **How do you think you could know if the Holy Spirit is helping you?**

Ask willing kids to share their answers to the last question with the entire group.

Say: The Holy Spirit does help us. The Bible tells us that the Holy Spirit is there for us, guiding us and giving us peace. The Bible also says that *the Holy Spirit helps you when you pray.*

Leader tip In this lesson, kids are learning about how the Holy Spirit helps us when we pray, but the Holy Spirit also does so much more. If time allows, consider talking about what else the Bible says the Holy Spirit does. In Luke 11:13 we find God will give us the Spirit if we ask. In John 16:7-15, the Holy Spirit is an advocate and helper. And in Romans 8, we read that the Holy Spirit helps us find truth and guides us.

Real-Life Application

Powered Prayers

Distribute a deflated balloon to each child.

Say: **We can inflate balloons and tie them. We play with them, use them to celebrate birthdays, and even fill them with water and throw them at people! Right now let's do something with these balloons you probably haven't done before: Let's imagine these balloons are prayers. In fact, hold your balloon in your open hand and think of things you'd like to pray for—help for a sick neighbor, thanking God for giving you food, or asking for forgiveness.**

Point out that their prayer balloons need air. Have kids stretch them out and start blowing while they pray for those things they just thought about. Don't let kids tie their balloons, just keep them pinched shut.

When kids finish inflating their balloons, say: **Imagine the air in your balloon is like the Holy Spirit giving power to your prayers.** *The Holy Spirit helps you when you pray.* **The Bible says that we don't always know what we should pray but the Holy Spirit does. In just a second I'm going to tell you to let your prayers go to God, and then we'll get an idea what it's like as the Holy Spirit gives power to our prayers. Ready? On your mark, get set, let your prayers fly!**

After kids let their balloons fly, have them collect their balloons.

Have kids form pairs. If you have an uneven number of children, join in so every child has a partner. Read the following questions out loud, one at a time, allowing a minute in between questions for partners to discuss.

- **How is the Holy Spirit like the air you put in the balloon?**

- **How does it feel to know that God wants to hear from you?**

- **How could this balloon help you remember that** *the Holy Spirit helps you when you pray?*

Ask for willing kids to share their answers to the last question with the entire group.

Say: *The Holy Spirit helps you when you pray*—just like the way you need air in the balloon to do anything with it, your prayers need the Holy Spirit.

Real-Life Commitment

Come Boldly

Have kids form new pairs. If you have an uneven number of children, join in so every child has a partner.

Tell kids to share with their partners about a time they received a special invitation; for example, maybe they got invited to participate in a wedding or go camping with a friend.

Allow three minutes. Alert kids when there are 30 seconds left. When time is up, have kids turn their attention back to you, and say: **God has given us so many good gifts, including the invitation to pray.**

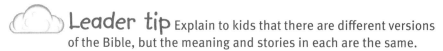 **Leader tip** Explain to kids that there are different versions of the Bible, but the meaning and stories in each are the same.

Read this version of Hebrews 4:16 from the New Living Translation: "So let us come boldly to the throne of our gracious God. There we will receive his mercy, and we will find grace to help us when we need it most."

Say: **God's invitation says, "Come boldly." What do you think someone who comes boldly into this amazing throne room would look like?** Let kids do their best impression of someone coming boldly into the room.

Say: **We don't have to tippy-toe into God's presence. We can barge right in and say whatever we're thinking about—and God promises that we'll receive mercy and grace to help us.** Explain to kids that mercy and grace mean that God forgives us for things we do wrong, even though we don't deserve his forgiveness.

Say: **We don't even need to know how to pray, or what to say, because God's Spirit will fill up our hearts with God's love and guide us. Let's practice.**

Have kids stand. Explain that earlier the kids bowed in respect to God but this time they'll practice talking to God boldly. Have kids close their eyes and imagine God's throne room with God the Father, Jesus, and the Holy Spirit all there. Have kids march in place as they imagine themselves marching into God's presence. Encourage them to keep marching in place, swinging their arms, and stomping their feet as they silently pray to God. Have kids tell him they'll count on the Holy Spirit for help, too.

Give kids about 30 seconds to stomp and pray. Afterward, bring kids back together and discuss the following as a group.

Ask: • **Why is it important to pray boldly?**

• **What are some ways you can spend more time in prayer?**

Say: *The Holy Spirit helps you when you pray.*

Colton's Challenge

Gather kids for a closing prayer. Explain that talking to God is as easy as talking to someone on the telephone. Tell kids to find a quiet space in the room and to spend some time talking with God. Have them imagine they are using a phone to speak to God, just as if they were talking to a friend.

Allow two minutes. Alert kids when there are 30 seconds left. When time is up, have kids turn their attention back to you. Have kids gather together again, and tell them that as you pause during the prayer, they will have an opportunity to add times they will remember to pray.

Pray: Dear Jesus, today we've learned that 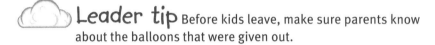 *the Holy Spirit helps you when you pray.* **Help us remember to pray when...**(pause for children to add times they'll remember to pray). **Help us to get to know you better as we spend more time praying and counting on your Spirit for help. In your name we pray, amen.**

Say: On your way out today, share with a friend or leader about when you promised God that you will pray. Also, take your balloon with you to remind you to pray.

Leader tip Before kids leave, make sure parents know about the balloons that were given out.

Three Simple Tasks

1. Jump up and down while saying the alphabet.

2. Take your shoes off and stand on one leg.

3. Squawk like a chicken.

Jesus Said to Believe in Him and Follow Him

Making It Real

Kids will discover that [✎] *Jesus said to believe in him and follow him.*

Objectives

Kids will:

✔ Learn that Jesus leads us in the right direction and won't let us get lost.

✔ Play a game that shows how Jesus can be at the center of our lives.

✔ Understand that believing in Jesus is the only way to heaven.

✔ Commit to following Jesus and telling others about how to get to heaven.

You'll need...

☐ several Bibles

☐ cotton balls (8 to 10 per child)

☐ a variety of navigational tools, such as a map, compass, arrows or signs, and an image of a GPS device

☐ 1 large yellow balloon, inflated

☐ smaller balloons, half red and half blue, inflated (1 of either color per child)

☐ paper

☐ pencils

☐ slips of paper, each at least 8-inches long

☐ washable markers

☐ 1 cardboard cutout in the shape of the letter *J* for each child, plus a few extras

☐ glue or glue sticks

☐ soft instrumental music and a CD player (optional)

What the Bible Says

 *John 6:39-40*

This Scripture tells about the heart of Jesus' earthly ministry. At the beginning of John 6, Jesus miraculously feeds a crowd of 5,000 people with five loaves and two fish from a boy's lunch. That evening, Jesus calms a rough sea and walks out on the water to his disciples' boat to assure and comfort them. The next day, crowds pursue Jesus, demanding miraculous signs. When they ask for "the true bread from heaven" that God offers, Jesus said, "I am the bread that gives life." That leads into the Scripture for this lesson.

Twice in John 6:39-40, Jesus mentions the will of God. It was God's will that Jesus would come to earth to die and rise again to save us from our sins. It's also God's will that none of the beloved children he's entrusted to Jesus would be lost. This brings to mind Jesus' description of himself—just a few chapters later in John 10—as the good shepherd who knows his sheep and sacrifices his life for them. Likewise, in the parable of the lost sheep (Luke 15:1-7), Jesus describes the efforts of a shepherd with 100 sheep to search for one that's lost. When the man finds the sheep, he rejoices greatly—just as God does in heaven when "one sinner changes his heart."

John 6:39-40, with its action verbs *believe* and *raise*, also echoes the familiar gospel-in-a-nutshell message of John 3:16: To live forever with God in heaven, all we need to do is believe in Jesus—no strings or conditions attached. To emphasize this wonderful promise, Jesus repeatedly uses the word "I" in John 6:39-40. "I must not lose even one." "I must raise them up." "I will raise him up." Jesus assures us of a perfect future and a life that will not perish. As John 14:6 says, Jesus is the only way to eternal life in heaven. This is great news to share with all of Jesus' little lambs: *Jesus said to believe in him and follow him.*

From Kids' Point of View

Early elementary-age children are beginning to distinguish between fantasy and reality. They're also starting to grasp the concept of miracles, symbols, and even God's nonphysical nature. Because of this, it's important to use age-appropriate words that allow children to practice their burgeoning logical-thinking skills. Otherwise, they'll get frustrated.

Children ages 4 to 8 begin to experience fear of the unknown, so they want to believe in a God who's all-powerful, all-knowing, and everywhere all the time. Their understanding of God's love, tenderness, and trustworthiness depends on how adults express these qualities. So you have an important opportunity to convey love, acceptance, and forgiveness to children.

Heaven can be a tough concept for children—and, indeed, for all people—to understand. Kids may have heard that certain loved ones are now "in heaven with Jesus" and have questions about heaven's location and appearance. They may wonder what people do in heaven, who gets to go, and how we get there. Point to the Bible's assurance that heaven is a real place without sin or pain, and tell kids that all people who believe in Jesus will go to heaven when they die.

Young Colton Burpo describes seeing "markers" on Jesus' hands during his visit to heaven. These markers were the nail wounds from Jesus' crucifixion, which Jesus showed the disciple Thomas after rising from the grave (John 20:24-29). Thomas had doubted that Jesus was alive and wanted to touch the wounds for himself. For many early-elementary-age children, too, "seeing is believing." They may relate to Doubting Thomas and need reassurance that Jesus and heaven are real, even though we can't see them right now.

For all his doubts, Thomas may also have been a tactile learner! Children who fit in this category prefer to touch and handle objects, experience the world, and act out events. Such interaction helps them make connections with big-picture concepts and abstract ideas such as faith and heaven.

In this lesson, your kids will learn that *Jesus said to believe in him and follow him.*

The Lesson

Get Ready

Before children arrive, create a trail of cotton balls on the floor that leads to your room. Then continue the trail throughout the room, placing various navigational tools along the trail. Put a Bible at the end of the trail.

Let's Get Real

Follow and Find

Welcome children and ask: **How did you find your way here today?**

Pause for kids to respond.

 Say: **I didn't want anyone to get lost, so I made a special path to our door. And look—it keeps going!**

Choose a child to be the leader.

Say: **Let's follow** (name) **along this special path to see what we can discover.**

As you arrive at each navigational tool along the way, switch leaders. To add a challenge, give each new leg of the journey a twist; for example, everyone must hop along the path on one foot.

Leader tip Children may be tempted to pick up pieces of the cotton ball path, which is fine. Eventually, you'll use the cotton balls to make the craft in the "Real-Life Application" section.

Have everyone sit in a circle, with their navigational tools in the middle.

Ask: • **What was it like to take this journey?**

• **What did you like or dislike about your responsibility, whether it was leading or following?**

Say: **Sometimes trails aren't obvious—or as easy to follow as this one was. I've been lost before, and I'm sure some of you have, too.** Tell briefly about a time you got lost.

Have kids form pairs. If you have an uneven number of children, join in so every child has a partner. Read the following questions out loud, one at a time, allowing a minute in between questions for partners to discuss.

• **Tell about a time that you were lost.**

• **Where did you turn for help, or how did you get found?**

• **What did you learn from that experience?**

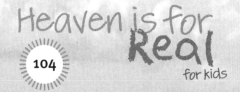

Ask willing kids to share their answers to the last question with the entire group.

Hold up one or two of the navigational tools and say: **Certain tools can help keep us from getting lost. We call these navigational tools.** Have kids repeat the phrase. **Tell me about these things and how they're used.**

Allow time for children to share their knowledge of and experiences with the various tools.

Say: **When you use one of these tools or follow someone who knows where he or she is going, you can be pretty confident that you'll end up safely at your destination. When we follow Jesus, he always leads us in the right direction so we won't get lost.** *Jesus said we should believe in him and follow him.*

Hold up the Bible, and say: **God's Word is a very special navigational tool that always keeps us from getting lost. Today we'll find out what the Bible says about how to get to heaven.**

Ask children to help you collect the cotton balls, and set them aside for later.

Leader tip Here's a different way to explain it to kids: When asking people for directions, you will get different responses. You can listen to what everyone has to say, but wouldn't it be best to get directions from someone who has been where you want to be? Finding heaven is a lot like that. Many people may say they know they way, but you can find out from someone who lives there! You can find out Jesus' directions to heaven in the Bible!

Making the Bible Real

Jesus said we should believe in him and follow him (John 6:39-40)

Get Ready

Beforehand, inflate one big yellow balloon and the smaller balloons, half of which should be red and half of which should be blue. Tape the big yellow balloon about six feet up on a wall of your meeting area. Place two empty buckets, one labeled Group A and one labeled Group B, on the floor underneath the yellow balloon, a few feet apart from each other.

Form two groups, and have groups stand on opposite sides of the big yellow balloon, facing each other. Give each child in Group A one small red balloon and each child in Group B one small blue balloon.

Say: **This game is called "The Sun at the Center." The goal is to be the first group to get all your balloons into your bucket. Here's the catch: The only way to get a balloon into a bucket is by first bouncing it off the big yellow "sunshine" balloon in the center. Once the balloons are in the air, you can't touch them again with your hands. But you can use the rest of your body to try to bump the balloons into your bucket. And it's OK to help the other team. Ready? Go!**

Play several rounds as time allows.

Afterward, read the following questions out loud, one at a time, allowing a minute in between questions for groups to discuss.

- **What made this game easy or difficult?**
- **What strategies did you use as you played?**
- **How were you able to help one another?**

Say: **This yellow balloon is similar to the sun in our solar system. This "sunshine" stayed in the same place, and our game revolved around it. Without this sun, you couldn't have followed the directions and filled your bucket.**

Have kids form a semicircle around the yellow sun balloon. Distribute Bibles, and have kids look up and read John 6:39-40, with readers helping nonreaders. Tell kids that in these verses, Jesus is explaining that he is the way to heaven.

Ask: • **How does the game we played remind you of a relationship with Jesus?**

After children respond, say: **Our lives depend on Jesus and need to revolve around him, just as our world revolves around the sun.** *Jesus said to believe in him and follow him. The only way to get the balloons into the bucket was to go through the "sun," and the only way to get to heaven is by believing in Jesus, God the Father's Son. Let's look closer at how we go to heaven.*

Heaven is for Real for kids

Real-Life Application

Following Our Leader

Hold up a cotton ball and say: **Cotton balls remind a lot of people of sheep—and especially little lambs. Earlier, you followed a leader along a trail of these cotton balls.**

Ask: • **When you're following a trail, how does it help to have someone to follow?**

Say: 📝 *Jesus told us to believe in him and follow him,* **and he calls himself our good shepherd. Let's read more about that.**

Have kids form pairs. Readers should partner with nonreaders. Explain to kids what a shepherd is and how shepherds take care of sheep. Have pairs read John 10:14-15. Then read the following questions out loud, one at a time, allowing a minute in between questions for partners to discuss.

• **How is Jesus like a shepherd?**

• **How are we like sheep or lambs?**

• **What are some ways we can follow Jesus?**

Ask willing kids to share their answers to the last question with the entire group.

Hand out the cardboard *J*'s.

Say: **This is a letter *J* for *Jesus*, but it's also the shape of a shepherd's staff, or crook. Shepherds use a staff to direct their flocks of sheep in the right way. Let's decorate our crooks to show that we follow Jesus, the good shepherd.**

Have children use markers to write today's Bible point on one side of the cardboard: 📝 *Jesus said to believe in him and follow him.* Help kids as needed.

Then have kids glue several cotton balls to the other side of the crook and decorate as they'd like.

Say: **Take your crook home and display it as a reminder to believe in and follow Jesus, our good shepherd.**

For this activity, you'll need cotton balls (8 to 10 per child), a cardboard cutout in the shape of a large *J* for each child, markers, and glue or glue sticks. Gather the cotton balls you used previously, and have extras available as needed.

Real-Life Commitment

Jesus Is the Way

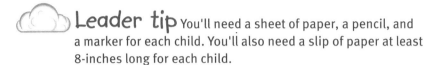 **Leader tip** You'll need a sheet of paper, a pencil, and a marker for each child. You'll also need a slip of paper at least 8-inches long for each child.

Distribute sheets of paper and pencils to children.

Say: **Because we've been talking about directions, let's try an experiment. Today you're going to be cartographers, or map-makers. On your paper, draw a map from your home to a special location—maybe your grandparents' house, your favorite restaurant, or even a fun vacation spot you've visited. Add any pictures or hints that'll help people who are using your map, so they don't get lost.**

Allow three minutes. Alert kids when there are 30 seconds left. When time is up, have kids turn their attention back to you. Ask a few willing kids to share their maps with everyone.

Leader tip You may want to let kids pair up and swap maps and try to remember the way. If they have trouble, you can remind them that Jesus is going to take us to heaven and you don't have to worry about the directions.

Ask: • **What made this task easy or challenging for you?**

• **What special clues did you add to your map to help travelers follow it correctly?**

Say: **Sometimes maps can be hard to follow. There might be a lot of streets to turn on, or maybe road construction will make you get lost. The good news is that the "map" to heaven is really simple. It never changes, and it's always trustworthy because it's in the Bible, which is God's Word.**

Have kids form new pairs. Readers should partner with nonreaders. If you have an uneven number of children, join in so every child has a partner.

Give each pair a Bible, and have one partner read John 14:6 and have the other partner read Acts 4:12. Have partners read their verses to each other, if both are readers. Help as needed. When pairs are finished, say: **Jesus is the only way to heaven. The map, or way, to heaven is simple: We need only to believe in Jesus. That's why** 🖊 *Jesus said to believe in him and follow him.* **Jesus also wants us to tell others how to get to heaven.**

Read the following questions out loud, allowing a minute in between each for partners to discuss.

- If someone asked you how to get to heaven, what kind of a map would you draw?

- What reminders or clues would you include so people didn't get "lost"?

Allow two minutes. Alert kids when there are 30 seconds left. When time is up, have kids turn their attention back to you. Then ask willing kids to share their answers to the last question with the entire group.

Distribute paper slips and markers. Explain that making a map to heaven is as simple as drawing one line. Have kids write the words *Jesus* and *Heaven* on opposite ends of the slip. Then instruct kids to draw a line from *Jesus* to *Heaven*.

Say: Jesus is the way to heaven. You can give your map to someone as a reminder that believing in Jesus is the only way to get to heaven, where we'll be with Jesus forever. You can help others to know that ✎ *Jesus said to believe in him and follow him.*

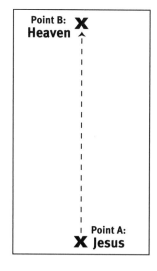

Colton's Challenge

Gather everyone for a closing prayer. Explain that when Colton came back from his trip to heaven, he wasn't shy about following Jesus and doing what Jesus asked of him. Encourage kids to be strong and follow Jesus in whatever he wants them to do.

Ask kids to find a place to sit and pray alone. Have them ask God for ways they can follow Jesus this week. You may want to have some soft music ready to play during this time. When the time is right, wrap things up by praying:

Pray: **Dear God, today we learned that** *Jesus said to believe in him and follow him.* **Thank you for sending Jesus to die for our sins so he can raise us up to heaven. Be with us as we follow Jesus, who is the only way to heaven. And help us tell other people about Jesus so he can raise them up to heaven, too. In Jesus' name, amen.**

Jesus Really, Really Loves Us

Making It Real

Kids will discover that 🖉 *Jesus really, really loves us.*

Objectives

Kids will:

- ✔ Find out what it means to be convinced of something.
- ✔ Learn that God's love has no end.
- ✔ Discover that nothing can get in the way of God's love for us.
- ✔ Make bracelets as reminders of Jesus' love.
- ✔ Commit to sharing Jesus' forever love with other people.

You'll need...

- [ ] several Bibles
- [ ] paper
- [ ] pencils
- [ ] a variety of measuring devices such as rulers, tape measures, and measuring tapes
- [ ] assorted magnets of different sizes and strengths (at least 1 per child)
- [ ] a variety of objects that represent love, such as a family photo, a valentine card, a flower, candy, and other mementos
- [ ] 20 glow-in-the-dark beads per child (available at craft and hobby stores)
- [ ] 20 red beads per child
- [ ] 8-inch length of string or twine for each child
- [ ] washable markers
- [ ] slips of paper

What the Bible Says

 *Romans 8:38-39*

Although the Apostle Paul became one of the most prolific writers and well-traveled missionaries of the early Christian church, he had his share of struggles. He had to live with the knowledge that he once persecuted Jesus' followers (1 Corinthians 15:9). He had to live with a physical "thorn" in his flesh (2 Corinthians 12:7-10). And, like all humans, he had to live with the tempting pull of sin (Romans 7:15).

But in the book of Romans, Paul moves from an exploration of sin and law into one of the Bible's most hope-filled passages. In chapter 8, he describes life in the Spirit, frequently using the words *peace, glory,* and *love.* The majestic closing passage asserts that people who follow Jesus have "full victory."

Paul lists the strongest foes and forces imaginable, but none of them stands a chance of keeping us from God's love. *"Jesus really, really loves us"* is a simple message, but children can't hear it enough. As they grow, they'll face new challenges and doubts. So it's essential to let them know God's love is so powerful that *nothing* can ever separate us from it.

From Kids' Point of View

Children often have interesting perspectives on the concept of love. Popular e-mail forwards contain cute quotes from the younger set. Some kids think that love is all hugs and hearts, but one 8-year-old wisely said, "When someone loves you, the way they say your name is different. You just know that your name is safe in their mouth."

Love and safety seem interchangeable for early elementary-age children. Routines are comforting because they help kids know what to expect and how to behave. In the same way, children appreciate a God they can always talk to, feel safe with, and be loved by.

Although children's fears may differ from adult worries, they're still real. Kids need to hear that even when bad things happen or other people let them down, God still loves them. His love isn't conditional or limited, and nothing can stop it, block it, or interfere with it. Assuring kids that nothing they face can ever separate them from God's love offers comfort for the present and confidence for the future.

When Colton Burpo woke up in the hospital and had recovered from his medical crisis, he recalled his last moments in heaven as Jesus telling him, "Colton, you have to go back now." His restoration to health was an answer to fervent prayers by Colton's family.

Among all the wonders Colton experienced in heaven, he insists the most important thing Jesus wants us to know is that he loves his people.

In this lesson, your kids will learn that *Jesus really, really loves us.*

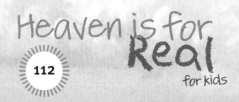

The Lesson

Let's Get Real

Convince Me

 Leader tip Throughout the activities, have older kids pair up with younger ones. The older kids can help their younger friends who may not yet be reading, or who may need help understanding certain questions.

Have kids form pairs. Readers should partner with nonreaders. If you have an uneven number of children, join in so every child has a partner.

Say: **Today you have an important challenge to tackle. I'll give each pair a slip of paper containing a statement. Your pair will have one minute to try to convince the rest of us that your statement is an absolutely true fact—even if you aren't sure about it or disagree with it.**

Give each pair one of the slips of paper you prepared in advance. Tell kids that they have two minutes to prepare their case. Alert kids when there are 30 seconds left. When time is up, have kids turn their attention back to you.

Then, give each pair one minute to present its case to the rest of the group.

Ask: • **How convincing was each pair?**

• **Describe what was it like to be a "convincer."**

• **How well do you think you proved your statement?**

Allow time for discussion. Explain to kids that it can be tough trying to convince people of something—especially when you aren't sure of it yourself. Tell kids it was a little hard to know whether some of these statements were true or not.

Say: **Today we'll hear some important words from Paul, who wrote parts of the Bible and told many people about Jesus. He was absolutely convinced that** *Jesus really, really loves us!* **Let's begin by taking a few measurements.**

Get Ready

Write a variety of fact and opinion statements on slips of paper. You'll need at least one statement for each pair of kids. Duplicates are OK. Here are some examples:

Gravity is real.

The earth is round.

Vegetables are good for you.

Math is fun.

Girls are more creative than boys.

Making the Bible Real

Measure Up (Ephesians 3:18)

Have kids form new pairs. If you have an uneven number of children, join in so every child has a partner.

Give partners a measuring tool. Have the kids use it to see whether they can tell the size of the following three items: someone's foot, a window, and a pencil.

 Leader tip Adapt the items to be measured according to your surroundings. Make sure the three items you choose can be easily measured, either by length or by width. Pair older kids with younger ones to make this job a little easier.

Allow time for children to measure. Then have a few kids share their results, noting which item was longest and which was shortest.

Say: **Very good! Now that you're warmed up, let's try some more measuring. Write down a measurement for the following three things: your attention span** (pause)**, your happiness level** (pause)**, and God's love for you. Ready? Go!**

Pause as children consider what to do—and possibly try their ideas. Even if they're perplexed, encourage them to come up with some type of answer.

Allow two minutes with a 30-second warning for kids to finish up. When time is up, have kids turn their attention to you.

Ask: • **What results did you come up with?**

• **Which set of items—the first or the second—was easiest to measure, and why?**

Point to the measuring devices and say: **With all these tools available, it seems we should be able to come up with measurements for anything.**

Ask: • **Why can't these tools measure things such as attention spans, happiness, or love?**

After children respond, say: **Paul, the same Bible writer who was convinced that** *Jesus really, really loves us,* **also wrote about the size of God's love. Let's find out what he said.**

Distribute Bibles to pairs, making sure readers and nonreaders are paired. Ask kids to find Ephesians 3:18. Ask for a willing child to read the verse while the others stand and stretch according to the verse.

Get Ready

You'll need various measuring devices such as rulers, tape measures, and measuring tapes, as well as paper and pencils.

Have the willing child read the verse aloud: **"And I pray that you and all God's holy people will have the power to understand the greatness of Christ's love. I pray that you can understand how wide** (have kids stretch their hands out wide) **and how long** (have kids reach out as far as possible) **and how high** (have kids reach up as high as possible) **and how deep that love is** (have the kids reach to the floor)**."** Ask the child to read the verse again as kids repeat the motions.

Say: God's love for us is so great that we can't put a specific number or limit on it. Human measurements aren't big enough to describe the size of God's love.

Ask: • What are some ways we might be able to see God's love for us?

• If someone asks you to prove that God loves you, what would you say?

Allow time for discussion, and then have willing children share their answers from the last question with the entire group.

Say: *Jesus really, really loves us*—a whole bunch! Not only is God's love bigger than we could ever imagine, but it's also more powerful than anything else that exists. Let's see just how powerful Jesus' love for us really is.

Real-Life Application

Show and Tell

You'll need a variety of objects that represent love, such as a family photo, a valentine card, a flower, candy, and so on. Choose other items that have special meaning for you as well. You'll also need red beads and glow-in-the-dark beads, plus bracelet string or twine. Make a sample bracelet ahead of time, alternating the red beads and the glow-in-the-dark beads on a piece of string.

Display your love-related objects.

Say: It's time for Show and Tell! Here are a few of my favorite reminders of people I love—and of people who love me. Hold up each item and briefly describe why it's special to you. Then have kids form groups of four or five. Each group will need at least one reader. Read the following questions out loud, one at a time, allowing a minute in between questions for groups to discuss.

- **Tell about some items that remind you of special people in your life.**

- **How can you tell when people *really* love you?**

- **When people show you they really love you, how do you respond?**

Give each group a Bible. Have one person look up and read 1 John 4:9-11. When groups are done, give kids paper and markers.

Explain to kids that there are many types of love. We love our pets, we love our families, and God loves us. Have groups come up with a poem explaining how God's love is different and why it is the best kind of love. Encourage kids to use parts of 1 John 4:9-11 in their poems.

Allow four minutes. Alert kids when there are 30 seconds left. When time is up, have kids turn their attention back to you. Then ask willing groups to share their poems with the entire group.

Say: Remember, 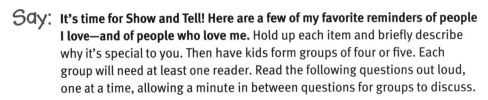 *Jesus really, really loves us.* He tells us all about his love in the Bible, and he showed us his love by dying on the cross for our sins.

Ask: • **How can you show and tell other people about Jesus' love?**

Give each child a piece of string and two small piles of beads. Hold up a completed bracelet and say: **Let's make a reminder of Jesus' love for us—and of the love he wants us to show to other people. The red beads remind us that Jesus died and came back to life again for us. The glow-in-the-dark beads remind us that we can "show and tell" Jesus' love to other people—especially those who don't know Jesus yet.**

Have children each complete a bracelet, alternating red and glow-in-the-dark beads. Help them tie the string or twine in a knot when they're finished.

Say: When someone asks about your bracelet, tell that person 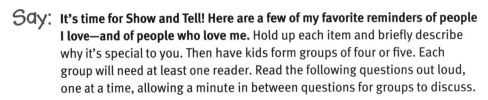 *Jesus really, really loves us!*

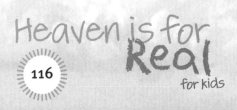

Real-Life Commitment

The Main Attraction

 Leader tip Your kids may wonder, if God really loves children, why do they get hurt? Remind kids of James 1:17-18. Between Satan, our bad choices, and living in a sin-filled world, bad things happen. But God doesn't hurt us, he helps us.

Set out the magnets. Have kids form pairs. If you have an uneven number of children, join in so every child has a partner.

Have each child choose a magnet, making sure partners get different kinds. Have pairs explore and see how well their magnets work together and which objects around the room do the best job of attracting the magnets. Walk around the group and ensure kids use positive and negative magnet pairs so the magnets don't resist each other. This is important for later.

Allow three minutes. Alert kids when there are 30 seconds left. When time is up, have kids kids turn their attention back to you.

Ask:
- **What discoveries did you make about these magnets?**
- **Which magnets have the strongest attraction or pull?**
- **Which items did the magnets stick to and not stick to?**

Allow time for discussion, and then give each child a slip of paper and a marker. Have kids write or draw a few things that scare or worry them. They can be big or small things. And tell kids they don't need to share them with anyone if they don't want to.

Allow two minutes. Alert kids when there are 30 seconds left. When time is up, have kids turn their attention back to you.

Say: **Lots of bad and sad things can happen to us on earth. People get sick, fight, and hurt one another.**

Have willing children share what they put on their slips.

 Leader tip Fears and worries can get personal, so don't require kids to share them. If no one shares, you can mention some of your personal fears and worries.

You'll need several sets of magnets of different strengths and sizes, slips of paper, and markers.

Magnet Warning

This activity uses magnets. Use only large magnets that can't be swallowed, and warn kids against putting a magnet anywhere near their face. A swallowed magnet is a medical emergency, so take steps to discourage kids from doing anything but the assignment with the magnets, and collect them when the activity is over.

Read the following questions out loud, one at a time, allowing a minute in between questions for partners to discuss.

- **Why do things scare people or cause them to be afraid?**

- **What kinds of fears or worries do you think might be too big for Jesus?**

- **How can you ask Jesus for help with those extra big worries and fears?**

Say: We learned earlier that Jesus' love for us is so great that we can't even measure it. Hold up some magnets. **These magnets aren't quite that powerful, but for now let's say they represent Jesus' love. Take turns putting your paper of worries between you and your partner's magnet, and let's see if our problems and worries interfere with the magnets' power.**

Give everyone a chance to experiment.

Ask: • **What happened to your fears and worries?**

• **How did those fears and worries affect the magnets—or Jesus' love?**

Ask willing kids to share their answers with the entire group.

Say: **No matter what problems we face, they can't interfere with or stop Jesus' love for us. Let's hear what it is about Jesus' love that convinces Paul so much.**

Have partners look up Romans 8:38-39. Ask a willing child to read the verses while others read along. Ask kids to keep their ears and eyes open for ways to finish this phrase: "Jesus' love is more powerful than..."

Say: **Paul lists some pretty big things in this passage. Yet none of them is strong enough to stop Jesus' love. Neither are your fears and worries. Just as these paper slips can't stop the magnets from sticking together, bad things that happen can't separate you from Jesus' love, because *Jesus really, really loves us.* That's something we can never hear too often.**

Colton's Challenge

Closing Prayer

Gather kids together.

Say: **Now let's close in prayer, thanking Jesus for his powerful, forever love.**

Have kids hold their hands up in front of them with fingers and palms pressed together. Then have kids think of one way Jesus shows his love to us, and with each thing they think of, they can bend a finger down, interlacing their fingers.

Allow two minutes for kids to finish interlacing their fingers. When their hands are clasped, lead the kids in prayer.

Pray: **Dear Jesus, today we heard that** ✏️ *you really, really love us.* **Thank you for this love—a love that's so big it can't be measured and like our clasped hands, keeps us close to you. Help us show and tell other people about your great love. Help your love live and grow in us. And always remind us that you are our forever friend who** ✏️ *really, really loves us!* **In your name, amen.**